Spread....... to Bedsheets

Simplify your finances

Transform relationships

Dream with confidence

Scott Cuyler

DEDICATION

To that girl from Coleman's Irish Pub, thanks
for that first dance and all the dances
since….hopes of many yet to come.

Table of Contents

How did we get here?

Now That We Found Love   **7**

The Inertia Dance   **16**

Finding the Starting Line   **28**

Make that change!

Step 1 – Stop Believing the Money Myths   **36**

Step 2 – Foundational Questions   **59**

Step 3 – Putting It into Practice   **83**

We're not going back!

The New Habit – Communication Is the Key   **110**

Enjoying Budget Love   **115**

Taking It to the Next Level   **125**

About Those Bedsheets   **130**

Now That We Found Love

"Money often costs too much" — Ralph Waldo Emerson

Now more than ever, couples need a simple but effective approach to managing personal finances and winning with money. The demands of our daily lives leave little time to focus on our finances. Living on credit and debt is a constant temptation, and technology only makes it easier to spend money. Couples need a framework and process that allows them to get the most out of their income. Too many great love stories are ending under the weight of out-of-control spending. This book is designed to help couples shift money from a source of stress to a force of unity. This book is not going to ask you to work harder but to instead simplify your finances and work smarter. In just a few hours each month, you can get complete control of your finances, transform your relationships, and ignite intimacy.

I wrote this book to teach individuals and couples to apply minimalist principles to simplifying their finances. Stop believing the "I just need to make more money" myth, and recognize that more money is not the answer until you maximize what you make today. Stop chasing 10 percent returns on your investments and retirement accounts while overspending and paying 20 percent interest on credit cards. Stop thinking the answer lies in some fancy personal finance software to manage your spending. All you need is a simple and consistent approach to manage your spending and maximize your income. The average couple spends more than 100 hours watching TV each month. Are you willing to spend a few of those hours planning and managing finances? Doing so will allow you to reduce your financial stress while feeling more connected to the one you love.

As the notorious RWE (Ralph Waldo Emerson) said, money can often cost too much. When you find love, create financial habits that help that love grow. Don't let out-of-control finances and money fights hold you back from a great relationship. I found love and spent years trying all the latest money-management approaches. The transformational moment came when I realized I was making this finance stuff much more difficult than it needed to be. Not convinced? Read the fine print. I guarantee that just a few hours a month spent getting it right with your financial spreadsheet will mean more quality time between the bedsheets.

So consider me your financial love coach, a cross between a financial advisor and marriage counselor. Since earning my MBA, I've spent time teaching, writing, and working with couples. My passion is identifying the common threads that enable couples to win with money. I've spent countless hours studying personal finance experts and thought leaders. I've even studied the financial lives of my friends and families. I've studied why people who make nearly identical incomes have such different quality-of-life standards and live with very different levels of personal financial stress. Like you, I read the headlines about once-wealthy movie stars and professional athletes going bankrupt. I've learned that winning with money starts with making it your servant instead of your master. Whether you make millions or thousands, you will not win with money until you get in control. Without a plan, money can often cost too much, with financial stress impacting relationships and standing in the way of pursuing dreams.

Beyond those around me, the person I've learned the most from is the one I see in the mirror each morning. I've been through a transformation that is waiting just around the corner for anyone struggling with their finances. Rest assured, the tools and processes outlined in this book are taken from many years of studying and teaching personal finance. This process works.

Although my academic background is in finance, my "street cred" comes from real-life experience. I've lived in a house for the past 20 years. Houses eat money. I have three beautiful children. Children eat everything inside the house that eats money. I have the joy of owning two cars. Cars burn money. Finally, I have done the marriage thing with an amazing wife for almost 20 years. My wife is the inspiration behind my time spent writing this book and speaking about the power of personal finance to transform lives. In the first few chapters of this book, I share some moments and experiences as a father and husband that forced me to reconsider my view of money and the need to gain full control of my income. Trust me when I say I would not have spent the hundreds of hours writing this book and building my website if I did not believe so deeply in the principles and strategies that follow. I am confident this book can provide one of the highest returns on investment of any book you will ever read. Yes, I know, you probably didn't pay a lot for this book and so the bar is not high. Forget the cost of this book. The real value is your time. The time you spend getting complete control of your finances will come back to you tenfold. This process has worked in my life and in the lives of many others whom I've had the chance to teach and guide.

This book is filled with specific and practical advice. I'm sure you and those around you will find something to disagree with. I implore you to keep an open mind. Watch out for well-meaning family and friends who suggest credit cards and spending your way to happiness is the answer. Getting the same "low" interest credit card they got to "fix" their financial problem is not the answer. I've even heard people in churches tell me they prayed about it, and God told them to stretch and buy that house that was outside their price range. There is no shortage of financial advice out there. Whether it is the sage advice of your brother, a well-meaning friend, or even the voice of God, always consider the fruit your financial decisions will sow.

As you begin to change how you manage your money, listen to that voice in your own head that knows you work too hard to be broke and under constant financial stress. There are very powerful forces that can cause great, smart, and wealthy couples to spiral into a financial mess. As much as you might want to jump into the nuts and bolts behind the process, a critical first step is to review the money myths and fundamental questions that follow. You need to examine how you think about your finances and what beliefs led you to where you are today. Winning at personal finances is not a prescriptive, step-by-step path that is the same for every relationship. Yes, I spend a considerable amount of time on the nuts and bolts of managing your finances, but the first step is to examine how you think about money and what winning will look like for you and the one you love. Finally, some of you are reading this book to help someone you love. Maybe a child or parent needs some help. This book helps equip you with the questions you can ask followed by the structures you can help your loved one implement.

As you begin this journey, watch for a common thread: Simplicity is key. You can try many different financial tools and software, but if you have three different checking accounts, five credit cards, and always answer "yes" when asked if you want cash back, you will never get control of your finances and should just hire a full-time accountant. Beyond keeping multiple accounts, constantly using credit to enable overspending will create a tangled mess. I'll get a few of you worked up by suggesting it may be time to stop playing the credit card reward points game. Ending your credit card addiction and stopping the reward programs can help you afford five times the number of "free" airline tickets. As someone who left credit cards behind several years ago, I can say I haven't missed them, and I'm going to do all I can to never go back. For some, the food analogy works. If you are trying to lose weight, should you load your cupboards with junk food? If you are trying to manage your money and simplify your finances, you need to be open to eliminate anything that complicates your financial life. You don't have to decide yet, but you need to acknowledge that simplifying a very complex financial picture is not possible without making some changes.

Winning with money is much more than building a great new spreadsheet. Too often, we feel stuck in a deep financial hole not seeing all the ladders around us. A great place to start is to learn what helped other people dig out of their financial mess. For many of us, we've followed a well-worn path into debt. The good news is there are paths that lead to a new reality where you are in control of your finances. Let's look at what has inspired others to change their ways and win with money.

It is critical that you, and if you are in a relationship, your partner, have a reason to change. I'll share what inspired me to change in the hopes that it may help inspire you or someone you love. Once you are on board and ready to change, I will challenge you to examine your thinking and debunk financial myths that hold people back from winning with money. Once we're clear on the myths, there are a few fundamental questions you need to answer prior to building your financial dashboard. These questions can help you understand how your current spending habits impact your financial world. We finish with the nuts and bolts of setting up and managing your dashboard, and my closing argument provides insight into the many bonus gifts and impacts this new process will have on you and your relationship.

As you move from theory into practice, this book provides you with specific tools and templates to manage your finances. Notice I did not say I will tell you how to spend your money or how to make more money. You need to walk before you run, and so your first step is to focus on managing what you make today. Winners control their finances; they know where they stand today and where they are headed. They simplify their money-management process and minimize the time they spend managing their money. They view their income as a way to invest in the people and relationships that mean the most to them. If you start this journey with the mindset that winning with personal finance is simply making more money, you need to stop and reread this paragraph. You cannot "out-earn" bad money habits.

As we are about to depart on our journey, I envision two camps forming. In the first group, everyone is excited to turn the page and jump right in. There is a second group looking at me with skeptical faces. A lot of people in this second group are dipping their toe in the water and looking to run away. Maybe your wife or partner asked you to read this book. You're reading but looking for the catch or heavy sales pitch to buy my new program. There is no program to buy, and I won't ask you to send me money. Although if you want to send me money, send away. If you are skeptical, focus on one word: desire. Why should you invest the time and energy in this money-management stuff? You need something that breaks you out of the power of inertia to not change. If you are not sure about this inertia force, stay with me through the next chapter. It is about a desire, a want to live a different way, a better way. You can radically change your financial future by turning the corner today, right now.

The Inertia Dance

*"So many fail because they don't get started,
they don't go. They don't overcome inertia.
They don't begin." - Ben Stein*

Inertia is the invisible force that explains why we humans just keep doing what we've been doing even though we know that we should change. I'll assume it has been a while since your high school physics days and provide a quick refresher on inertia. Newton's first law of motion states that an object at rest stays at rest while an object in motion stays in motion with the same speed and in the same direction unless acted upon by an unbalanced force. Said another way, objects, including you and me, tend to keep on doing what they have always done until there is some significant event or experience that makes them change their behavior.

Newton understood that it is the natural tendency of objects and people to resist change. What does Newton's law and inertia have to do with your finances, you ask? Quite simply, you are going to avoid getting control of your finances until a significant force or experience prompts you to change. That event can be simply reading this book and realizing you're missing out on enjoying the money you work so hard to make. Maybe you are spending too much time worrying about finances and relying on your overdraft account. It could be a call from a debt collector or realizing that your children are nearing high school age and college tuition is approaching quickly. It could be sickness that impacts your income or your job is eliminated. If you find yourself in the middle of one these events, hold on tight and keep reading. If you are not in crisis but still living paycheck to paycheck, now is the time to put a plan in place that allows you to build a reserve that can help your bank account and relationship weather the storm.

You heard from Sir Isaac Newton so now consider Sir Cuyler's law of financial inertia. My law states that financially stressed people will continue to live on the edge until Life Happens and you need a better plan. Inertia can also work in your favor, as once you get control of your finances and enjoy the calming sense that comes from confidence in your financial plans, you will not want to go back. You will continue to do the things that helped you get control. Use this inertia force to your advantage. You need to get into a new habit, and that means committing to this process for several months. In our house, we've been living these principles for about ten years, and

17

we will never go back to our old ways of managing money.

So what changed for me ten years ago? What were the inertia-breaking moments that changed our life and led to this book? I'll share these experiences in hopes they inspire you and possibly connect you with similar moments in your life.

The first experience was a chance to learn about a special child who attended a local school. It was a warm spring day, and the first-grade class was abuzz with laughter and fun. Everything seemed to be normal except just outside the classroom door, a child was sitting alone crying in the hallway. If you happened to pass by that boy, you would surely think he was there because he made a bad choice. The story was much more complicated. The chair was placed in the hallway for that child as an accommodation to help the young boy find some space to process through his feelings. I learned that this boy had recently found out that his parents were getting divorced, and the chair was a place he could go to cry and gather himself away from the staring eyes of his classmates. What does this boy sitting in the hallway have to do with your personal finances?

First, know that I'm not sharing this story to pass judgment on divorced parents. I know there are times when divorce can be the best answer albeit

18

difficult for all involved. What I am passing judgment on is allowing financial stress to pull a marriage apart and having children impacted because mom and dad didn't make managing their finances a priority. One of the most common reasons couples cite for relationship stress and divorce is out-of-control finances and debt. Studies have shown that money and financial stress can tear the fabric of marriage, cause communication to break down, and force people to grow apart. Couples need to recognize the destructive power money stress has on their family.

Society continues to make it very easy to get into financial trouble, while social pressures can cause people to hide and ignore these financial problems. Your Facebook feed is a daily reminder of what other people just bought and all the fun you are missing out on. Now more than ever, couples need to be dedicated to a reality-based financial communication plan. My process forces you to communicate about finances. It is designed to help solve financial challenges early before they grow into large marriage-crushing weights. Financial decisions are a vital topic for constant communication and healthy couples challenge each other, working together to allocate their finite income. When financial stress begins to creep into relationships, it likely happens on smaller purchases and decisions regarding spending. If couples are not on the same page, the bills will show up in the

19

mailbox and the lack of money to pay expenses can cause great couples to fight or worse, to avoid the situation and just use more credit. Credit comes with interest, and interest is a new pet that must be fed every month. Once you create an "interest pet," it eats your income, taking away your ability to get ahead of your expenses. These financial stresses can drive wedges into relationships and begin to erode the foundation of the relationship.

That boy sitting in the hallway personified the pain and disappointment that results from marriages breaking under financial stress. I believe in the power of love and want you to grow and cultivate that love. But, and this is huge, you are not immune to the destructive forces of financial stress. Don't believe you and your partner are gifted at the art of bearing massive financial stress. The weight of financial stress leaves too many adults devastated by the end of a relationship, not to mention little kids crying themselves to sleep wondering why mom or dad doesn't live at their house anymore.

A few years after the boy-in-the-hallway incident, I encountered my second significant financial experience in the men's room at work. It was a normal work day at a large bank in downtown Boston. As I entered the restroom, a coworker in his mid-thirties was preparing to exit. He was a friend so we engaged in the usual light discussion topics that fall within the acceptable men's restroom genre. He commented on a rumor that I was dating someone at work, and so I reciprocated by asking how things were with his family.

This normally jovial coworker said he wasn't doing so well. He shared that his marriage was falling apart, and it was obvious he was hurting. He went on to reveal more details, and a few of his words have stayed with me since. He spoke profound words for a bathroom conversation. He said, "We just stopped communicating." He shared that they did love each other, and I could tell in his voice and his body-language that he loved the woman he was divorcing. His advice was when the going gets tough, don't stop communicating, don't build walls. Emotional walls can be so strong that neither member of the relationship can reach the other person and marriages can crumble. I'm confident I haven't had a more profound conversation in the men's room since. If you follow what I teach in this book, you are forced to communicate about how you spend your money, and those decisions will inform every other part of your life together.

Beyond the obvious benefits of getting complete control of your finances, there are several hidden gifts waiting to be revealed in this journey. The first hidden gift is revealed when you work together to get your finances in order. If you spend a few hours a month planning your spending, you will find you're reviewing your calendar and communicating on what your priorities are in the upcoming month. Whether it is an upcoming weekend trip, a birthday party for a friend, or school expenses for the kids, every expense is an opportunity to stay connected on what is happening over the next few weeks and what you need to allocate your income to. What starts as a financial discussion always helps you stay in sync on your calendar and where you will be spending your time. Effective communication is the key, and this process ensures couples stay connected both on the dollars and their calendar.

Beyond the two stories I shared, there was one more significant event which is the reason this book exists. At the age of 40, I thought I understood poverty through reading books, watching movies, and travel. Nothing prepared me for that first August day in the Dominican Republic. I had traveled to a remote area of the Dominican Republic with my family on a service trip. My role along with my two boys, aged 7 and 9, was to help run a baseball program at a local park while my daughter and wife helped at a local school. We were in a remote mountain village that did not have clean drinking water or a reliable power grid. Service trips always start out about wanting to help others but end up changing the way you view the world and your own life. My ten days in the Dominican Republic truly changed my life.

On day one, my boys and I boarded the back of the truck rambling down a dirt road headed to the local sports field. There we were, no seat belts, rolling along through the small village, just watching the locals going through their morning routines. You could say we were far outside our comfort zone of suburban Connecticut. We arrived at a dusty and worn-out baseball field. We had a fun morning playing baseball with twenty boys from the area and then took a break for lunch. My boys and I grabbed our packed lunch, sat in the shade, and devoured the food. My two boys finished their lunch and threw their brown paper bag lunches into the garbage as they headed back onto the field to play. At that moment, I saw hunger eye to eye as one of the local boys was hiding around the corner. He was waiting for my boys to throw out their bags so he could pull them out of the garbage and eat the leftover scraps. My eyes met his, and I came to understand the incredible power that flows through my hands and my bank account each month.

I couldn't believe what I saw and over the next ten days and struggled to consider what my response should be to such a massive need. How were boys the same age as my sons not provided with basic needs and what should I do about it? Fast forward to our last night on the service trip. We sat as a group of fifty people on a warm evening with the lush mountain landscape in the backdrop as our trip leader asked us to consider the question that I'll pose to you. What is holding you back? We were given a small piece of paper and asked to write a word or two that described what would hold us back from making a difference once we were back in our comfortable homes. What one or two words summarize why I can't make a difference? My answer was the title for this chapter: inertia. For me, and I suspect for many of us, it is the feeling that we are stuck in the demands of our day-to day-life. We know there is a need but struggle to see how we, just one person, can make a difference. I wrote down the word inertia as I knew I would probably just keep doing what I was doing, living the busy life. That evening, this book was born as I set a goal to not only get my finances in order so our family would make a difference, but I also knew I could multiply the impact if I could help others organize their finances and create breathing room to give and support those in need.

The boys I worked with over the ten days, their smiles and their hearts, helped me look beyond my own selfish concerns to realize I am incredibly blessed to live in an area that has clean water, reliable power, good schools, and many positive role models. I went from a position of feeling sorry for myself and the financial pressures I faced to understanding the

24

incredible gifts and prosperity I was blessed with. To this day, I get emotional thinking about each of those boys. I realized I was making too much money to be living with the financial stress I had brought upon myself. I decided that I needed to get full control of my finances, and I needed to make a difference. The term transformational is overused, but it the best way I can explain this experience. I came back a changed person with a clear hurdle in front of me. I couldn't keep doing what I was doing and expect to win with money. I had to overcome inertia!

We started this chapter noting that inertia explains why we resist change. You are going to need some experience and unbalanced forces to break you out of your current habits. A few takeaways from the two stories I shared: first, don't underestimate the wisdom that could be found from listening to people going through a divorce, even if it is offered during your next trip to the restroom at work. Second, respect the corrosive force financial stress can have on a relationship. Overspending, not being in control of your finances, and living under constant financial stress can leave two lovebirds arguing about the credit card bill instead of enjoying a night together.

As I close this chapter, there may be a few of my fellow men (and ladies) thinking "he's going over the top, a bit extreme with these stories of kids crying in hallways and relationships ending." Don't use my stories. Look around for your own examples. You probably know great people and couples who have struggled through financial stress. As I meet people and teach these principles, I'm convinced we have an epidemic of couples living under massive financial stress. My approach will not eliminate financial stress. No process or plan will. What it will do is put you squarely in control of your finances and give you communication tools that ensure money stress doesn't destroy your relationship.

Where will the desire come from in your heart? Inspiration is probably closer than you think. You don't have to travel to the Dominican Republic to find those much less fortunate. I'm confident you can look around your community and connect with people struggling with the impact of poverty. If it isn't poverty, find inspiration when your new baby is born or when that baby is grown and headed to college. I am often inspired when I read about a single mom who dreams of starting her own business at home only to make that dream a reality. Maybe you work for a company, and you never quite feel secure about your job. Be inspired to take control of your financial future. Downsizing happens to great people, and you owe it to yourself and your family to have a financial plan that gives you and your family choices. Living paycheck to paycheck and not having emergency savings creates stress. Find inspiration in going to work knowing that if the announcement is made that your plant is closing, you have the savings that gives you choices as you take the next steps. The economy will go through difficult recessions, jobs can be eliminated, and medical emergencies do happen, so find inspiration in having a plan and resources to make it through the difficult times. It will not happen unless you commit to managing finances this month, this week, and most importantly, today.

It is time to look ahead to building the foundation for your financial plan. This foundation starts with evaluating how you view money and approach your financial decisions. What follows are some lessons and simple steps you can take to transform your personal financial life. The change and improvement require you to walk down a new path. This is a well-worn path that leads to a place of financial control. Consider this book a guide to help you get through the transition to a new way to manage your finances. Don't let inertia win. You can change!

Finding the Starting Line

"If you don't know where you are going, any
road will get you there." – Lewis Carroll

Lewis was on to something as living without a financial plan is like heading on a trip without a GPS or map. The self-help shelves of your local bookstore are filled with rows of books on personal development and tips on how to get started. Not surprisingly, studies consistently demonstrate that successful people invest time to develop a plan and even write that plan down. How about you? What feelings come to mind when you think about formulating a few of your key financial goals? I've put a lot of thought into why most Americans don't have specific goals when it comes to their finances. I think the answer is simple and best demonstrated with a brief story.

Picture yourself at the local marina stepping aboard a new sail boat. As you step onto your new boat, you notice three dime-size holes in the bottom and water starting to leak in. Luckily, you have a bucket nearby and start bailing the water out. You tirelessly use that bucket to bail water out of your sinking boat. As you are doing this, I come along and ask about your plan to sail to the island just beyond the horizon. What is your reaction? It is the same reaction when someone asks about your long-term financial goals. You are so busy trying to stay afloat today that contemplating long-term financial goals is a waste of time. I need to keep living paycheck to paycheck, and someday, I'll get enough money saved to start thinking about my future. We have neither the time nor the energy to make long-term financial plans when all our energy is spent bucketing water out of our sinking boat. Only after you repair your boat and the water stops pouring in, can you look up and begin to plan your journey to the island.

Some of your stories are a little different. It could be that you make enough money so you don't notice the small leaks. You make $100,000 a year and that is enough to be wasteful and not really have to watch your money closely. You make enough that you can defer thinking about a long-term financial plan, assuming the money will be there when you need it. This book is just as much for someone struggling to make ends meet as it is for the couple floating by with enough money to be wasteful and not really paying attention to the details.

Now for the second hidden gift. Managing your personal finances effectively over the course of several months begins to reveal a path to reaching long-term financial goals. By managing your money this month and next, you begin to give yourself space to define bigger and more distant goals and dreams. We all know people who retire only to feel lost and stripped of that which they believed defined their value to society. Don't let that happen. When you plug the leaks and your financial boat is comfortably floating, you will look up and see new horizons. The conversations that are part of this financial process naturally begin to bend toward long-term thinking. The reason you struggle to define a goal and plan is because you are not confident that future can happen. This is a great point to counter what our culture says about budgets as tools only for boring and predictable people. I argue the opposite. Budgets open doors and create pathways to new opportunities you might have thought never possible.

Now back to Lewis and his quote at the top of this chapter. In what may seem a contradiction, I'm going to suggest many of you should procrastinate defining exactly what your long-term goals are. If you are someone who has very clear long-term goals, go ahead and jump to the next chapter. For the rest of you, hold off trying to layout a very detailed financial long-term goal. Start with a simple and universal goal such as "Our long-term financial goal is to have choices." This goal is to be in control of when you retire and decide what you do in that retirement.

I was fortunate to have parents who encouraged me to save in my 401k retirement account from very early in my career. Even with a commitment to my retirement account, until I had complete control over my finances, long-term goals were not something I thought about. Today, I am confident my dream of spending some part of my retirement years living on a sailboat and cruising the southern oceans will be a reality. I know my life may change so I always come back to my simple goal. I want to manage my finances today, this week, and this month so I can have the freedom to make choices when I retire. Visualize where you are headed but don't put pressure on yourself to have it all figured out.

Now it is your turn. Don't leave this chapter without capturing your goal. This is step one. If it is late in the evening and you are ready to go to bed, take this one step. Write down your long-term goal! Wake up tomorrow morning knowing you have started on a journey that will make that goal a reality. Don't spend hours wordsmithing. Keep it simple, and don't use a lot of fancy words. Feel free to steal this basic but aspirational goal. "We will get complete control of our finances to redefine our incomes as the engines that not only help us reach short-term goals, but also allow us to dream big!"

If you are facing significant struggles with your finances, it will be very hard to consider a goal beyond just paying the rent next week. Don't despair! As you work through this process, you will begin to create some breathing room. As the months pass, new doors will open up and you will begin to see paths that lead toward your goals and dreams. I wrote this book to offer a lifeline to those in financial trouble. Start with defining a goal that inspires you. You can do this!

If you are in your twenties, having a goal matters. If you are in your sixties, I don't have to tell you that this goal matters. It doesn't matter how old you are, having a goal matters. With your goal written down, you can move to the next phase of the journey. Now it's time to challenge how you think about money and your personal finances. Does your current method of managing your finances work? By "working," a financial system is successful only when both people in a relationship feel confident that they know where their money is going and know it is going to the things that matter most.

If both of you lay your head down at night and are confident you have control of your finances and plan, please give this book to one of your broke friends. Let me be clear. The last thing this book is meant to be is a prescription for how to spend your money. My goal is to teach you and your partner how to communicate about money so that you can spend your income on the things that matter most to you. Having a plan is about bringing the right priorities into focus so you don't finish the year and wonder where the money went.

Before we move to the next step, what about those people reading this book who are not currently in a relationship? Whether you are thinking about getting into a relationship or recovering from a relationship, this financial management can help you find happiness and prepare you for future relationships. I am sometimes asked if it is easier to get your finances in order when you are married or single. If I ask my married friends, they say it would be easier to get my finances in order if it was just them. Ask those who are single, and they often say it would be easier to fix financial issues with two incomes and a partner to help keep them accountable. The grass is always greener, so let's focus on the grass on your side. If you are married, you have a partner to work with but you also need to prioritize and compromise. If you are single, you call all the shots, but you also might want to invite a friend or family member into your process to encourage you and keep you accountable. This process works for couples and for singles. Being single and being mature about your finances, are the markings of a person I would hope most people would want to meet. Single and out of control financially does not bode well for combining finances down the road. This book is written for those in love, looking for love, and anywhere in between.

Now for those in a relationship, an important disclaimer you need to read: In working with families, couples, and individuals, I've found the process of getting your personal finances in control is incredibly rewarding, but it also can be disruptive. This new approach to managing your money will put financial realities in clear view, giving you the power to make decisions and get the most out of your money. This sounds good, but you need to proceed with a healthy respect for this disruptive power. If you are in a relationship where financial topics or behaviors are a concern, please consider working through these changes with some additional support. The goal of this book and my program is to build stronger relationships and families, not to put them over the edge. Be prepared that this program can push you out of your comfort zone. It is essential to pace yourself, love one another with conviction, and hold each other up as you put these new processes and tools in place.

You may want to hang out on this point for a bit. Speaking from personal experience and hearing from others who have taken the step you are taking, there is wisdom in considering the forces you are about to mess with. This force is the same force that you may have experienced when you start any transformation: you are going to upset the status quo. For many people, their current money-management system would be what many financial consultants would refer to as a "dumpster fire." That said, it is your system so you'll defend it and take offense when someone criticizes it.

If you do this money stuff right, you will be forced to sit down and discuss your future. You will need to prioritize. Unlike the government, you cannot just print more money so a word of caution on your first few budget meetings. They will not be easy, and you may disagree about where the money will go. Be prepared to compromise and stay focused on the prize: your relationship and a shared sense of control. As someone who has followed the process for almost ten years, it gets easier every month to the point where you look forward to the budget meetings and the sense of connection you have with your partner on priorities.

On to the next step of the journey. It's time to explore some common money myths.

Step 1 – Stop Believing the Money Myths

"We can't solve problems by using the same kind of thinking we used when we created them." - Albert Einstein

Albert's quote highlights the need to rethink how we've been thinking about our personal finances. So you've just finished defining your basic financial goal. What's next? If you are like me, you are tempted to take off running toward that goal. Before you start setting up your first financial dashboard, evaluate these money myths to find out if the software running in your head needs an upgrade. What follows are a series of financial myths that when unpacked, reveal practical advice to transform your personal finances. These myths are often paths to deception and lies that distract us from getting the most out of income. Consider this section as mental packing before your new financial journey.

A note before you read the first myth. Each of these myths is best served as a discussion point for

you and your partner to consider. If you are in a
relationship, review the myths together.

Six Money Myths

1. I just need to make more money.

2. Only people living paycheck-to-paycheck need to
plan their spending.

3. Math is the problem.

4. Planning your spending takes the fun out of life.

5. We're too busy to spend time managing our money.

6. Money can't buy you happiness.

Myth 1 - I just need to make more money!

Let's start with the mother (or father) of all personal finance myths. This deceptive thinking is the reason wealthy people go bankrupt. Debunking this myth is the path for bankrupt people to become millionaires. Financial stress is not caused by a need to make more money. Financial stress is caused by a lack of control of what you make today. This concept is so critical to understand that it bears repeating. Your level of financial stress is less about making more money and really about controlling what you make and spend today. Ask the person making $400,000 a year but using credit cards just to make ends meet or the couple making $40,000 but living within their means. It starts and ends with control. If you continue to live beyond your means and focus on what a friend or family member makes, you'll never find satisfaction.

Make no mistake: you should continue to try to make more money as you progress in your career. I hope you make millions, but don't go to the trouble of making millions if you can't manage your money and control your spending. More money and out-of-control finances lead to bigger problems, more guilt, and more shame. The key to effectively managing your finances is to balance your spending with your income. Until you manage your finances today, this week, and this pay cycle, adding more money to an out-of- control situation does not reduce your financial stress.

Time to reveal another hidden gift. This gift is revealed in your next raise or birthday check from your favorite aunt. When you are in control of your finances, you feel and appreciate incremental raises and unexpected gifts. If you are out of control, the 3 percent annual raise blends into the chaos of your finances, and you never appreciate the additional income. Maybe it was bigger than a small raise, something like your last tax return that was already spent before you had the check in your hands. There are endless examples that debunk this myth. You must stop thinking "I need to make more" and focus first on controlling what you make today.

This new way of managing money will help you apply more of what you make toward that which is most important to you. Many people who implement this process immediately find extra money that was previously slipping through their hands, from carrying debt and paying interest to paying $3.95 ATM fees. If one or both partners in a relationship are out of control with spending, there will be no peace and happiness come payday. Once control is established, you decide which direction you go. You will stop saying things like "Where did it all go?" or "How did we spend that much this month?" Instead, you will have a financial dashboard that will show you exactly where your money is going.

Easy credit is everywhere, allowing too many Americans to bury their head in the sand. Spend more than you make this month, just put it on the credit card, and go with the "we'll figure it out later" financial plan. Financial websites like CNBC.com and businessinsiders.com estimate credit card companies will send out more than 3 to 4 billion credit card offers each year.

Don't miss this next hidden gift. It took me a long time to see this one buried in this personal finance stuff so get in real close and consider the following question. Does constantly living on the financial edge impact your ability to make more money? When you are in debt and living paycheck to paycheck, you can't afford to take career risks. Taking a leap in your career becomes too risky. What if it doesn't work out or maybe you need to get past a short-term decrease in income as you ramp up in your new sales job? When you stop living so close to the financial edge, you can take that leap into a new job, use some savings to start a side business, or invest in someone else. These opportunities can help you make more money and eventually build wealth.

Still not convinced that being in control is more important than just making more money? For my closing argument, I offer hundreds of lottery winners. Lottery winners wake up one day, and their checking account has millions of dollars in it. Study these people, and an interesting trend is revealed. Lottery winners who can't control their finances end up broke. I hope you win the lottery, but more importantly, I hope you get complete control of your finances before that big check hits your account. Which person will experience more happiness and long-term satisfaction? Jack makes $70,000 a year and manages it well while Jill wins the lottery and is out of control with her spending. I think Jack wins. The turtle will win that race, and in many cases, the race doesn't have to be that long before the lottery-winning rabbit has burned through all the money.

Don't flip this page without considering the power of lying in bed at night and knowing you are in control of your finances. Being in control of your money reduces your stress level and may even help you relax and get a better night's sleep. You often hear a phrase that keeps many people awake at night: too many Americans are living paycheck to paycheck. My premise is that you don't have to live paycheck to paycheck. If missing a paycheck means you can't pay your bills, you are broke and you need to make some changes. Walking the personal finance tightrope so that the slightest slip means you fall deep into a hole filled with debt and stress should make you want to start setting up a net below you.

Please do not wait on a politician, family member, or friend to tell you to stop living paycheck to paycheck. Leave this first myth knowing that changing this pattern is not the job of the government, your parents, or someone other than who you see in the mirror. So many Americans choose to live in constant financial stress and crises. Decide today that you don't need to live like them.

Every time you sit down to review your
finances and plan your spending, you will have more
wants than money to pay for them. A financial
dashboard is not just for those living on the financial
edge. All couples should meet to communicate and set
their financial priorities. Regardless of whether you
are deep in debt or flush with cash, you need to plan
your spending. Maybe you are like most middle-
income Americans. You make enough money to waste
a lot of it, allowing undisciplined money management
to sacrifice financial goals and dreams.

I was in that last category. We made enough
money to mask sub-optimal money-management
practices. My biggest challenge was time. I was very
busy and needed to find a way to simplify finances.
What I realized in the mountains of the Dominican
Republic was profound. I never fully realized how
wealthy and lucky I was to live in America. I went from
feeling sorry for myself as I dealt with the usual
financial stress of raising a family to realizing how
fortunate I was to live in a country where we had
clean water, reliable power, good schools, low
unemployment, and finally, banks that only charged 4
percent on long-term mortgages.

It is time to reveal another hidden gift. As you work through the first six months of this new approach to managing your finances, you will begin to see new opportunities for returns on your investments. By investments, I'm not referring to just interest or capital gains on your retirement account. It took the wake-up call in the Dominican Republic to realize that taking full control of our finances would not only help us maximize our own financial health, but we would have enough money left over to invest in lives of children beyond those that lived in our house. When we struggle financially, we become very self-centered. We focus just on our own needs and in the process, miss amazing opportunities to get control of our finances and make a difference in this world. You have the power to change lives, and this unexpected gift emerges as you see someone or something you love in need. Having some savings and cushion in your bank account allows you to respond when the need arises.

Andy Stanley, one of my favorite teachers and one of the finest communicators I've ever heard, suggests a simple question we should all ask: what breaks your heart? The answer to this question is where you need to invest after you get full control of your spending. Most of us won't be able to fix that entire problem, but be assured that you can make a difference. Maybe it is a specific group of children in need, a social cause, supporting a faith community, or maybe it is the plight of dogs or abandoned pets at your local animal shelter.

Not sure you can afford to help? Assume for a moment that you are an average American family. Being average in America means you send your credit card company over a $1,000 in interest each year. That is more than $80 dollars a month you pay to borrow money. What if you could reverse the debt cycle?   The average family could change a lot of lives and make a big difference in our world. In the next ten years, that is $10,000 dollars. Getting your finances in control helps you invest in the things that matter most.

Myth 3 - Math is the problem.

The third myth is the easiest myth to bust. It says that personal budgets don't work because the math is too complex. To win with finances, basic math is all you need. Put away the calculus textbooks and uninstall those complex financial software programs. To succeed, you need to understand basic math. Some addition, subtraction, and we might mix in a bit of division. Winning with money has little to nothing to do with your capacity to do math. Still not sure if you have the math skills needed? Ask any 6-year-old to solve this math question. Three people end the month each with a different amount in their bank account. Person A has $100, Person B has $0, and Person C has $0 in their account and a $100 balance on their credit card. Who is doing a better job of controlling their finances?

I've worked with a lot of individuals and couples, and with 100 percent confidence, those struggling to control their finances and win with money can solve the math test with ease. The real question is "Do you know where you finished last month?" Were you like Person A, B, or C? Was it an exception month where the unexpected expense caused you to end up like person C? You need a system of communicating and tracking your personal finances that cuts through the financial fog, allowing you to see your financial health clearly. If you implement the process I outline, you will always know where you stand financially. I'm not suggesting this new process eliminates all money worries. It won't, but I guarantee you will know where you stand each month and you will know how you got there. The alternative continues to be just spend money when you want or need and wander through the month hoping you have enough to the pay the rent.

A last point on this myth comes from common marketing messages you hear from investment firm commercials: you just need to build an investment portfolio. Experts on TV and radio, friends and families, and even some financial advisors will suggest you just need to invest. I want to be clear: I'm not offering any investment advice. What I'm selling is a new way to think about your finances. Consider a gymnastics analogy. I'm partial to gymnastics as the first thirty writing sessions for this book were at my daughter's gymnastic club. Have you ever watched a new group of 6-year-olds start their gymnastics training? The financial advice we often hear equates to taking the new class of 6 year-olds and having them try backflips off the balance beam. We are bombarded with messages from investment companies encouraging us to open an IRA or invest in new mutual funds.

Don't get me wrong, I want you to have investment accounts, but step back for a minute and check the math. Before you start throwing money at investment accounts, get your income and spending under control. Show you can finish each month in the positive. So many couples I talk with are fighting to make a 10-percent return in their retirement accounts while overspending each month and paying 18-percent interest on their credit card balances. This isn't about you not understanding the math! You simply don't have a plan and are going by feel.

Before you jump to the next myth, let's review. It isn't about making more money but getting control. Planning your spending should happen regardless of how much money you have. Now we move forward knowing math is not going to stop you from winning.

Myth 4 – Planning your spending takes the fun out of life.

You can't make me. I'm not going to do a spending plan. Life is short, carpe diem. I'm not going to waste my time updating spreadsheets, and who has time to track every penny.

This book and my passion for teaching and helping others win with money is a result of the power I found in killing this myth and the corresponding thinking that so many people continue to adhere to.

Being out of control with your spending and stressing about money is no way to seize the day. By all means, live for today. When today, which was yesterday's tomorrow, arrives, face the day confidently and enjoy being in control financially. Go with Kramer's advice: "Serenity now, Jerry, serenity now!" I've done living today with financial stress, uncertain if I should be spending the money in my pocket. I couldn't tell you if I was making progress toward my long-term goals. I couldn't see through the fog of unorganized finances to focus on a long-term vision for my life. Once you get complete control over your finances, you'll have less financial stress, which should equate to a higher level of enjoyment for the day ahead. Carpe diem is knowing you are winning financially. A spending plan is also called a budget or financial dashboard. For many, the word budget invokes negative connotations. For a lot of those reading, a budget is just another way to take the fun and spontaneity out of life. No and NO!

A spending plan helps allocate your income into buckets so you have limits on what you can spend in each area and still be able to pay your bills. If spontaneity means spending your way into a mess, then you need to redefine spontaneity. When you allocate $100 to clothing this month, then you decide what you spend that $100 on as you shop. You are not walking into the store and loading up a second cart because the sales associate offered you a great discount for using their new store credit card. If I'm wrong and you really miss that sinking feeling when you open your credit card bills, then by all means, go back to overspending and being spontaneous. I am confident you won't miss the scary credit card bills and shame you feel from being out of control with your money. Flip the narrative and recognize that planning your spending enables you to allocate money to what means the most to you. You can be spontaneous but you need to do so within boundaries.

Next time you hop in the car to go to a new destination, cover your dashboard and turn off your phone map software. My guess is you will still get where you are going but you might run out of gas, you'll get lost, and it will take you twice as long than it should. The financial dashboard you are going to build and manage will give you the freedom to make financial decisions. It can give you the ultimate freedom to meet your long-term financial goals and allow you to chart your own path. I will concede that the math is boring, but the emotion, the peace that comes from being in control is awesome. Control brings peace and opens the door for better relationships and a happier tomorrow.

Unfortunately (or maybe not), humans can't just make more time in the day. We can, however, maximize the time we have. For purposes of this myth, I'm going to assume you would prefer to watch your favorite show over sorting and categorizing financial transactions. Time well spent managing your finances has a financial return and should actually be saving you time that you used to spend worrying about money. A financial plan that is designed for you and your family is a time saver. You can either proactively plan and direct where your money goes or deal with financial emergencies at the worst times. Ever find yourself at work trying to log into your bank and move money around to avoid bouncing a check? Busy people can't afford not to do a budget.

Many Americans are "too busy" to manage their finances. Work, family, or the latest binge worthy show doesn't leave time to manage finances. The result of not making financial planning a priority can be a profound regret as one approaches their retirement years. You will hear people say that they didn't make enough money. The reality could be they did not plan and control where their money went. If you don't make time to manage your finances while you are busy working, you can end up working much longer than you had hoped. It is never too late to get control of your finances.

Consider the reason why you think you don't have time to develop and manage a financial plan. This line of thinking is exactly why you should start your new plan this month. In our house, we have been updating our financial dashboard twice a month for almost ten years. I now spend less time managing finances and worrying about money than ever before. To win with money, you need to have two meetings on your calendar every month. These meetings should be scheduled within your pay cycles. As I show in the next chapter, most couples can get complete control of their finances by committing ninety minutes a month to updating their dashboard. For most couples, the first of the two meetings is the longest and should take about an hour. This is the pre-pay-period planning session where you are closing out last month's spending plan and deciding how you'll spend your income for the next month. The second meeting is typically a mid-month check-in to ensure the spending plan you laid out in the first meeting is staying on track.

What is more important: knowing who was voted off the island for your favorite reality show or your relationship? This is a simple question, but we live in a busy world filled with so many options for spending our time. You need to make it a priority to develop and track your financial plan. Once you have the process in place, the habit is there, and you can walk through each day with confidence and control in your personal finances. Depending on how much financial clutter you have, the first few months are likely going to take more time. From experience, don't schedule your meetings during times you are likely to be hungry, tired, or worse, hangry. Find a time that works for you both. For us, the Thursday night before we get paid is the night we selected. This is not about forcing the conversation when we're exhausted. That said, failure to block time on a consistent basis will yield inconsistent results. Couples who have consistent checkpoints on their calendars where they formulate their plan and talk about financial priorities will get the most out of this process.

For the first three months, you're going to need some extra time. Depending on how many accounts you have and how readily available your statements are, the setup should take about three to four hours. I'll share more on the details, but you should plan to spend time building your plan from the template on my website.

Beyond the financial stuff, you and your partner will discover that these financial conversations help you get organized for the month ahead. You can't discuss allocating your income without discussing what is most important to you as a couple. Thus, you end up not only planning your spending but likely will finish the meetings with clarity on the most important priorities over the next four weeks. You don't always agree on where the money will go, but commit to compromising and finishing every financial checkpoint with a plan. As a couple, coming to an agreement on how to spend your income is one of the most critical success factors in a marriage. You will be forced to look ahead 30 days and consider how much you are giving to your nephew for graduation, how much you are adding to your vacation fund this month, and whether there are any one-time expenses in the next 30 days that you need to set aside for. Is it August and do we need to increase the clothing spend this month for back to school? Do we have long drives planned and need to increase our gas allocation? For busy couples, the budget meetings help you avoid surprises during the month and keep you in synch on upcoming birthdays, commitments, and events.

Let's be clear on myth 5. Either make time to plan how you spend your money, or you'll waste a lot more time trying to unravel a financial mess. If you don't make time to focus on your finances, you are going to add a lot of financial stress into your relationship. The relationships with the people you love are too important. Make time in your schedule to manage your finances.

Managing your money can indeed bring you more happiness. Try finishing the month with your bills paid and some money deposited in your savings account. Think about what that savings means to you and your relationship. When you live on the financial edge, the constant threat of not being able to pay your bills and trying to keep up impacts your happiness. When you have savings, that positive balance in your savings account should bring you happiness. For couples, savings equals relationship insurance.

Consider the scenario where life happens and the washing machines dies. When you have savings, you call the repair technician and get the washing machine back up and running. When you don't have savings, you argue with your partner about who overstuffed the washer and debate who spent too much money on shoes last month all while the washer doesn't get fixed. You not only are stressed about how to pay for the repair, but you are now in fertile ground for a fight. Your finances are impacting life between your bedsheets. Not convinced? Think bigger than a broken washer.

What if the rumor at work is job cuts are coming, and your group is going to be impacted. You need to have a financial plan that includes building a financial buffer, a cushion for the unexpected. Once you step back from living on the financial edge, I'm confident you will not want to go back. Having a buffer becomes more important than the next trip or new TV.

For some of you, it is too difficult to see through the fog and stress of your current situation to really envision what it would be like to finish the month with your bills paid and some money left over. Don't let this distract you from debunking this myth. Rethink what having money left over at the end of the month can mean. Take some time to put savings into real terms for your specific situation. Here are a few examples, but feel free to make up your own. You are thinking of starting a family and know you'll have more expenses. Maybe you want to get a dog but know pets can be expensive. Do you live away from family and need to have money for emergency travel? Last-minute airline tickets are not cheap! Maybe your current employer is going through changes, and you want to ensure you have enough money to buy time to find a job in your area. Your check engine light will go on again. Consider your own specific situation, and define the things that can keep you up at night. Savings is the antidote to those concerns, and having a savings buffer can buy you happiness. Redefine what savings means to you and your relationship.

For many others, the challenge is that you never had anyone sit down and help you create a structure for managing your finances. You want to know where to begin or how to slow this fast-moving river of money down just enough to get control. You are not at the brink of collapse, but you've seen some people who seem to have their finances in order. Maybe you saw them step into someone's life at a time of need and provide financial assistance. Winning with money will not happen with the "spend by feel" approach. That is a recipe for debt and financial stress. This book is that lifeline, the step-by-step guide to managing your money today, this week, this month, and this year.

So, as you finish challenging these money myths, consider the Einstein quote we started with. "We can't solve problems by using the same kind of thinking we used when we created them." With new thinking, we move onto the work of building your own financial dashboard. To do so, we'll start with some fundamental questions everyone should ask prior to building their first financial dashboard.

Step 2 – Foundational Questions

"To know thyself is the beginning of wisdom." – Socrates

Before you can get to the nuts and bolts of living your new financial life, you need to know who you are dealing with. What follows are four fundamental questions to determine how you will approach building and managing your financial plan. These questions are at the heart of how to go beyond math and spreadsheets to a fundamentally new connection to your finances. The good news is Socrates already gave us the place to start with these questions: the man (or woman) in the mirror. If we jump in without understanding how we have related and thought about money, we can't reshape our own thinking to win with this new process. Take a few minutes to discuss these questions as the answers are the key to sustainable change.

The windshield or the rearview mirror?

Do you currently drive your financial car using your rearview mirror or looking through the windshield? Most couples I meet are experts at driving into financial stress using solely their rearview mirror. You'll know if you are one them by the type of money conversations you have. Do you get to the end of the month and wonder where the money went? If you spend most of your time and energy "managing" your finances by looking backwards, this next section is critical to internalize before proceeding to building your first dashboard.

The rearview mirror drivers are great at finishing the month and asking why is the credit card balance so high and what happened to all the money we had in our checking account? There is no easier and faster way to financial stress and money fights than hosting your own "where did all our money go" meetings. To win with your finances, you need to focus on the month ahead before it starts. Love yourself and your partner enough to pledge to rip the rearview mirror off the windshield. Before you say your situation is unique and you couldn't possibly predict the next four weeks, you have to stop telling yourself convenient lies. Within the first three to four months of following this process, you will be amazed at how well you can predict your spending with extreme accuracy. In fact, after a few months, you will be able to predict exactly where you are most likely to overspend and deviate from your monthly plan.

You might wonder why so many people in our country get away with driving their financial plans looking backwards. If my amazing grandmother was still with us, she would give us a loving slap to the back of the neck and say, "It is credit, you dummies!" We live in an economy that pushes credit. From clothing stores, gas stations, airlines, home improvement stores, travel agents, car dealers, plumbers, mortgage brokers, and just about every other business, interest from credit is an important part of how companies make money. Wherever you shop, you are asked by friendly staff if you want to sign up for the store credit card and spend money you don't have. Companies make it easy for you to worry about it later. Don't get me wrong; most of the companies are fine institutions run by good people. This has everything to do with the choices you make and nothing to do with the clerk offering you the credit card. They are doing their job, you do yours.

Consider the example of walking into a store and seeing an amazing shirt on sale for $35.00. You buy the shirt, but you are not sure if you had the money this month to pay for the shirt – a textbook rearview mirror financial move. Now assume you are about to buy that shirt when the cashier offers you 10 percent off if you sign up for the store credit card. You decided to get the 10 percent off, save $3.50, and then get to the end of the month unable to pay the full amount due. You do what most people do and pay the minimum, starting down the path of paying many times more for the shirt. This isn't the story of some evil marketing person, a politician, or your friend who told you that you looked awesome in the shirt and you just had to buy it. Own the decision and recognize that you are responsible for how you spend your money.

Stop working harder and start working smarter. Stop trying to manage spending across five store credit cards and two checking accounts. When you overcomplicate your finances, you take the joy out of purchases. You drive home from the store, unsure if you actually had the money to pay for the latest purchase or worse, knowing you used one of your credit cards and deciding to figure out how you'll pay the bill at the end of the month. The easy way is spending ninety minutes a month to plan and track your spending. Focus on the windshield and decide what will happen to your money over the next month, versus looking back on where it all went. Buy that shirt only when you know you had set aside some income this month on clothing, and you still had that money left to spend. Enjoy spending your money instead of living with buyer's remorse and the stress that comes with it when you get the credit card bill.

Winning with finances is not about deconstructing where the money went. I was the one in the relationship who was convinced the rearview mirror approach was the key to managing personal finances. I would download all our transactions at the end of the month, put them in categories, and pore over reports making fancy charts and graphs. Do this at the end of every month, and you set yourself up for a monthly argument with your partner. The money is spent, and all that is left is either to celebrate the amount saved or more likely, argue about where it went. We all know how easy it is to overspend so it is time to try a new method. Most couples try to control spending after the money is spent. Good luck with that, and don't be surprised if every time you talk about money, you are trying to sort out a mess. Planning where your income will go is what successful couples do. Finish the month knowing where the money went because you planned your spending and followed through on your plan.

When you start this process, there is no guilt, blaming, or worse, gloating. The essence of a forward-looking financial discussion is you taking control of the things you can control. For many, money and their finances are out of control, and maybe their lives are out of control too. The decision to start this process and look ahead for thirty days, plan for expenses, and agree to have a reserve or cushion is a profound change in thinking. This process moves you from a place of reaction to a place of planning and control. But what about the unexpected expenses?

Two key points regarding unexpected expenses. First, you need to have a reserve or at a minimum, a plan to create one as quickly as possible. To live without a savings buffer is to live on the line only to be pushed over that line when the unexpected happens. Second, you need to stop and ask yourself what your definition is of "unexpected." If you go to get your car serviced and the mechanic tells you need new tires, this is not an unexpected expense. Tires don't last forever so start a car repair fund and contribute a little bit each month. How about your dad or mom's birthday, a family member getting married, or more commonly, your friends inviting you to go to dinner? When you are honest with yourself, there are very few expenses in the next thirty days that you could not have planned for in your financial dashboard. We'll get to the specifics on how to do that in the next chapter.

A last but essential piece of making a real change requires couples to let go. If you share your life with someone who is good at holding a grudge, it's time to move on from past financial mistakes. We've all made bad financial decisions. If we're going to move forward and win financially, don't allow the baggage to hang on and undermine your ability to win. If you or your partner made a dumb financial decision, note the lesson learned, the desire to be better, and go forward to win together. As you start this process, agree that you are where you are and don't waste another minute going back over old territory.

For those who are married and in debt, work together to pay that debt off. For some couples, this is not going to be easy. Maybe one of you came into the relationship with a lot of college loan debt or maybe some significant credit card debt. Whatever it is, you need to decide that you are truly a team. I'm going out on a limb and guessing a few couples reading this book uttered the words "for richer or poorer" to one another some time ago. Commit to starting a forward-looking budget and throw that rearview mirror away.

Lastly, what do you do if your partner is not interested in participating in a new way of managing your finances? You need to do your homework and connect with your own "why." Why are you willing to change? Share that why with your partner and ask them what their "why" is. Redefine winning financially within their "why." Maybe you share the same why, but be open to finding other reasons and goals that resonate for your partner. Focus on what the benefits mean in terms of what they value. Let them know this financial stuff is important to you. If they refuse to participate, consider tapping into professional relationship support. Be persistent, but keep the tone focused on becoming a stronger couple rather than passing judgement or using threats.

Time to simplify. The key to spending less time on finances and more time enjoying your income is to avoid over-complicating your financial dashboard. Said another way: we need to be willing to change how we track and spend money. Answering yes to the cashback option at every store and sliding your debit or credit card five times a day is going to make it nearly impossible to track your spending. Be prepared to try some new ways of spending, or you will not succeed on this journey.

To that end, consider whether technology makes it easier to manage your personal finances? Before you embark on the financial dashboard building, define where technology can help you win and where it is your weakness. Online banking makes it easy to track your spending, but be careful not to confuse "track" with "manage." Technology makes it easier to spend money and yet, technology can be a double-edge sword so learn to handle it carefully and use the sharpest edge of the sword to cut through your financial complexity. Technology also has enabled us to spend money today and not feel the impact of that transaction until the end of the month when the bill comes due. Marketing professionals have a great term for this: purchase friction. Apple Pay, Alexa voice purchases, and the Amazon dots are all great examples of making it easier to part with your money. Research has shown that making it easier and faster to purchase a good or service can increase your likelihood of making that purchase.

Studies have shown we are likely to spend more when using credit instead of cash. Take a moment to consider the ways you prefer to spend money: credit, debit, cash, PayPal, whatever your tool or app of choice is. We all know it is only getting easier to click on your shopping cart. I'm convinced some day a generation will ask why they put those pictures of carts with wheels in the corners of websites. Grandpa, tell me the story again how you would push a cart through the store when you wanted to buy something!

So many of us finish the month and say, "I can't believe we spent so much money." Great companies, organizations that I admire and spend my money with like Apple, Amazon, and other companies that start with the letters B thru Z, pay their best and brightest employees to find new ways to make it easier for you to spend your money. Offering cash back after a purchase or no interest and no payments for twelve months are examples of reducing purchase friction.

I love technology, and I am proud of many of the American firms that pioneer these technical advances and marketing programs. I love capitalism, and I'm not here to judge these companies. The message is that you need to be in charge of you. Too many people blame others for their bad financial decisions. Time to take full control and commit to not allowing another sales person to define what you can afford. You should walk into every financial interaction knowing what you can afford and where your limits are. Don't buy the next house, car, or bag of groceries without knowing if you really have the money to pay for it.

As you start this new process, you need to recognize one of the biggest challenges that will stand in your way of getting control of your finances. Do the math. Just four transactions per day generate about 120 transactions a month. You will be overwhelmed with noise and confusion trying to make sense of 120 transactions a month. You need to simplify your spending and financial account structure. So, listen carefully. If you are not willing to say no to cash back, if you are not going to consider limiting the number of accounts and credit cards you use, you will never get control of your spending. You will be overwhelmed with noise and confusion wasting hours each month trying to figure out which bucket each transaction should go against. When I work with couples, this is the mud in which most get stuck. Are you willing to change how you spend money? I'll show you how in the next section.

As discussed early in the book, the force of inertia can make it hard for people to change their behavior. We're seeing an interesting trend where Americans are embracing a simpler life. Shows like Tiny House Nation feature couples embracing the minimalist lifestyle. While I don't advocate moving the family into the shed, my approach to finances is a simplified strategy that will de-clutter your financial world. Don't underestimate the behavior change and how attachments to our existing ways can undermine your success. I've met couples who have tried to manage their finances across three credit cards, five bank accounts, and stashes of cash in the cars, freezer, and the sock drawer. Before you go any further, agree that a financial process that is de-cluttered and simplified increases your chances to win. In the previous section, you agreed to stop being focused on the rearview mirror, but don't forget that at the end of every month, you must ensure that what you planned to happen, did happen. De-cluttering your finances equates to managing your income and spending in a few accounts. Less is more!

So how does one simplify and reduce the amount of transaction activity? One of my favorite simplification examples addresses the common caffeine addiction. I, like many of you, enjoy coffee and have a favorite coffee shop near my office. For a given month, I would swipe my debit card twenty times generating twenty transactions to track when we have our month-end check-in meeting. Throughout the month, I was never sure how much I had already spent on coffee so I just keep swiping.

A new and simpler approach calls for setting a coffee spending plan for a given month. Let's assume you set a $50 spending plan. On the first visit of your financial month, you walk in and use your debit to buy a gift card for $50 or better yet, you use the store's mobile app to replenish your account. Each time I purchase coffee, I check my debit card or app and by the second week of the month, my balance is only $10. That tells me I need to slow my coffee purchases. Either that or I need to increase my coffee allocation the next month. For most people, budgeting would probably mean writing down $50 on coffee and then keeping tabs of how much you spend, watching your debit card transactions. By the end of the month, you might have twenty-five debits for a given thirty-day period. By adding $50 to your coffee card or your mobile app, you go from twenty-five transactions down to one, and you can track your spending every time you purchase a cup of coffee. This is working smarter not harder.

The coffee example can work on all types of spending. From gas to home improvement store cards, you can set a budget target for a given month. Each month, you put the set amount on a gift card or that store's mobile app to significantly reduce the time you spend managing your finances.

So we've covered the role technology plays in making purchases but what about that moment you first decided you needed something? Beyond making it easier to spend money, there is a much subtler but powerful role and technology is playing with your finances. Before Facebook, if you wanted to compare what you had to the neighbors, you had to peek through the blinds. Today, Facebook has eliminated the need to snoop and with a click, you can see all the great stuff, amazing trips, and perfect lives of your social circle. Don't underestimate the power of social media and peer pressure to make you think you need to have it all today. "Comparison is the thief of happiness," is a great quote that is important to consider as you decide to try a new approach to managing your personal finances. Great couples need to set financial goals for themselves, and I'd challenge you to start with putting your relationship at the center of all your financial decisions. Forget what kind of car the neighbors just purchased (or should I say agreed to pay for over seventy-two payments at 7 percent interest).

What does winning look like for you financially? Stick to your plan, and don't let your

Facebook feed dictate your spending decisions. Again, I'm a big fan of Facebook and this isn't about them. This is about you and how you get yourself in that place where you just have to have something. Worse, we just bought that something a few months ago and our friend bought the new version and we get fixated on the need to upgrade. Slow down and monitor how you react to what others have.

We started by asking how complicated you want to make this financial stuff. My guess is you already feel it is very complicated or you wouldn't be reading this book. Let's finish with two key points. First, use technology to your advantage and don't let the new "easy" pay technology undermine your ability to control spending. Notice the word control appears here again. The second point is to stop focusing on what the other people in your life have and turn that energy inward to focus on how you can get your finances in control and achieve your own dreams. Don't be surprised if you find you thought you really wanted to buy something but change your mind after you begin to feel how much better you sleep with a financial cushion. When you can stop checking your checking account balance to make sure you don't bounce a check, you will not be missing the stress and angst of living on the edge.

Next, we will focus on the question credit card applications should have in large bold letters at the top.

3. Have you named and claimed it?

This is a profound and transformational question. What are you chasing? If you are out of control with your spending, living under too much debt, and stressing about your finances, what are you running after? As noted in the previous section, it has never been easier to compare what you don't have while overlooking how fortunate you are. Whether you make $30,000, $300,000, or $3,000,000, we live in a society that bombards us with what the next level of income has to offer. You feel the pressure to upgrade your home, buy the next model up on the new car, or purchase the latest phone. We are bombarded by marketing designed to feed the need for more stuff!

This section is about interrupting that voice in your head calling for more. Claim that voice and tame the desire. Don't misunderstand me. I want you all to be making more money, but until you get your spending under control and maximize your current income, adding more money often only makes a bigger mess. To name it and claim, I again lean on the wisdom of one of my favorite teachers, Andy Stanley. Andy puts into words the tension that I have wrestled with since my first weekend at college when I signed up for my first credit card while walking through the student center. Visualize in that moment the tension between "I want" versus "I owe."

The "I want" is a willingness to accept that I'm going to have to wait, and I can't have the thing I want since I don't have the money to buy it today. The "I owe" is that feeling we get with a credit card. "I owe" is the feeling you wrestle with at the end of the month, and it is the force behind a lot of financial stress. I don't want to wait any longer so I'm going to buy that thing using someone else's money and I now "owe" someone for lending me the money I didn't have today.

The key behavior change is to ask the question: What is worth the "I owe" in your life before you are emotionally entangled with a purchase?

Start with the basic definitions. The "I want" feeling is something most of us feel multiple times every day, even every hour or minute. You have that running list of stuff or experiences you want to have. Keep in mind, "I owe" comes with interest. You no longer fend off the "I want" feeling, but you used someone else's money and that someone else gets interest or money for the right to use their money. A simple example is you WANT a new house and purchase that house with a $200,000 thirty-year mortgage at 5 percent paying $20,000 down. The cost to live in that house before you pay for it is an extra $167,000. That $167,000 is the cost to stop "wanting" and living in that new house.

Hear me loud and clear: I'm not against getting a mortgage. Successful couples are very careful to only pay interest on the highest priority needs. They also put considerable time and effort to get the lowest interest rate anytime they borrow money. Using our house example above, if they were able to get a 3-percent loan, they would pay $93,000 in interest, saving more than $75,000 dollars.

A good place to start is to list what purchases you have made in the last few years that fall into these categories. When did you decide you would wait until you have the money, and when did you use credit? House and car payments are common examples of large purchases that we often pay for with other people's money. The average American uses credit cards and doesn't always pay the balance off. Looking back over the past few years, you will likely see you have been borrowing money to pay for dinner at restaurants. Maybe it is your stop at the mall where you purchase clothes and shoes on credit. The other big category is trips and vacations. My point on this list is not to judge but to make sure you are naming it and claiming it. It is very common to use other people's money to purchase houses and cars. But what if you put your next trip to a restaurant on a credit card and don't pay off the entire charge at the end of the month? You have decided to purchase a pizza with money you don't have, and that adds stress and pressure to your finances. You cannot win with money by consistently spending money you don't have. Interest on your debt will pile up, and debt will eat away at your ability to get control and get ahead of your spending.

The next step is to create one of my favorite lists. It's time to capture your envy list. This is the stuff you really want to buy but are willing to wait until you have money to afford it. You will have to wait, and that can cause envy as you see others have what you want. Know that waiting can be hard, but if you don't have the money to buy it, name that envy, claim it, and tame it by putting it on the list. This list can include specific items or even just a generic category like vacations, clothing, and house improvement projects. If you commit to proactively managing your money, I believe you can grow your wealth and reach levels you probably don't think possible. Cutting the line and using other people's money to get there today is a recipe for financial and relationship ruin.

Take this time to look at the two lists you just created and see what they say about your financial self. Agree on what things you think are worth taking on debt for. What do you want but are willing to remain in the state of a wanting? Compare your lists with your partner, and come to agreement on what should go on each list. Until you have your first financial dashboard, you really won't know what you can afford and how the interest payments you have today are impacting your finances. Your financial dashboard will point out what power interest has over your life.

Interest is something that should peak your interest. Interest is real money, and the dollars you pay each month to avoid feeling envy. For a lot of couples (and our government), too much interest* undermines your ability to pay your bills and worse, generate enough savings to create some financial cushion in your life. I need to emphasize that there isn't a right answer on where you should fall on the spectrum of want versus owe. What is essential is to make that decision before you walk into the store, shop for the new car, or go to the mall. Don't decide at the cash register or as the car saleswoman is having you sit in the new car. Know that your family, friends, sales associates, and financial advisors will offer their own advice on using credit.

That new riding mower or a new deck can easily be financed with a home equity loan. How about a new boat, truck, vacation, or maybe it is just a decision you'll make in the few hours like where we go for dinner. Let's hope the easy decision is to agree you shouldn't finance a pizza but push harder and challenge if there is anything else worth paying more for than what it costs. Look closely at your recent credit card statements, and you may find you are still paying for that dinner you ate three months ago. For many, the source of financial stress is a failure to set boundaries and pre-decide that you will no longer buy things on credit that you do not need.

To finish the name it and claim it section, ask yourselves what couple or family you want to be. If you have children, think about the messages you are sending them. Are you going to be the family of "no payments for twelve months," "same as cash," or "the seven-year car loan?" Or will you be the family that celebrates purchasing things with their own money while openly talking about having to save for other more expensive things? This may come as a surprise, but I know so-called "financial experts" who encourage people not to pay off their mortgage so they can deduct interest from their taxes. I hear about the financial "benefits of car leases" or why it makes sense to take that second mortgage out to add the pool! For purchases big and small, you need to start deciding not based on what the sales associate or your friend says but what the math means for your financial situation. Don't underestimate your confidence and happiness when you stop living on the financial edge and begin to create a financial buffer for you and your family.

4. Can we afford our lifestyle?

We've come to final question before we jump in and start building your first financial dashboard. This is the question most people prefer to ignore but one that must be asked and answered. What if your first dashboard is finished and it is screaming back at you that you don't make enough money to cover your expenses? Said another way: what if you can't afford your lifestyle? The good news is that you're in control now, and you can make decisions to fix the situation. The alternative is to just bury your head in the sand and go get another credit card. Reality will catch up to you. Today is the day to face the question, and the next chapter is going to help you see your finances in a clear and simple format.

Let's face the worst-case scenario where your expenses exceed your income. Your dashboard will give you a concise view of all the data you need to decide where you need to make changes. It will clearly show which expenses are the key levers you need to pull to get your budget in balance. It also might lead you to some big financial decisions. From downsizing to a smaller apartment or selling a car, your dashboard will give you the clarity you need to get control of your life. If you get nervous just thinking about these types of big changes, don't forget they are all decisions that can be reversed. If you decide to reduce your expenses and end up not enjoying being in control of your spending, there will be many options for you to turn back and go deeper in debt. I'm confident if you get your spending in line with your income, you will begin to feel a sense of calm and serenity that will motivate you to continue down the path of financial success.

Go deeper and decide as a couple why you think it is worth the time to invest in your personal finances. For my relationship, the answer was about freedom and choices. We wanted to control our personal finances so we had the freedom to decide if and when we wanted to change paths in life. We wanted to be able to give back, and we needed to know we weren't wasting money on things that didn't matter. Bringing the focus in a bit closer, we knew we wanted to worry less about our finances and focus more on enjoying the fruits of our hard work. When you spend time during the day without a clear plan, you waste a lot of time wondering if you can pay all your bills. You spend more time feeling sorry for yourself and waste a great opportunity to help someone or something else out in this world. There is a better way!

Now let's put it all into practice.

Step 3 – Putting It into Practice

*"If you don't know where you are going,
you'll end up somewhere else." - Yogi Berra*

Building Your Financial Dashboard

It is time to create your first dashboard. Be patient as this first version is the most difficult. Block several hours to collect, organize, and analyze your latest financial data. Spread the work over multiple days and sessions. To make the first iteration easier, I've broken the step into three sessions.

Before you get started, you should download free copies of the templates you will be creating. Go to www.scottcuyler.com and check the templates section. Based on your feedback, we'll be constantly improving the templates so read the update notes on my website to be aware of any changes since you purchased this book. If you have feedback, email me your suggestions. Now on to the first session.

The first step in building a dashboard is to create a list of all your financial accounts. The list should include ALL your financial accounts. This includes savings, checking, and all types of credit cards, auto loans, school loans, any other credit accounts. A good way to confirm you have listed all your active accounts is to pull your credit report at www.freecreditreport.com. There is no charge, and you'll immediately get a report containing all your financial accounts. The report will also include closed accounts going back seven to ten years so read the report carefully, and only include active accounts. For couples, make sure you download a free credit report for both of you.

Start with my account inventory template and list all your accounts. As you list each account, assign one of three types:

1. Core Account - used for depositing paychecks and paying bills
2. Expense Account - types include credit cards, auto loans, mortgage, rent, line of credit, a loan from mom and dad
3. Investment Account - any account used to save and invest money in

For all expense accounts, note the payment frequency and the normal or average payment amount. Add the interest rate for all expense accounts and the most recent balance. After you have a complete list of financial accounts, you need to list all other bills that you pay. List the bill and note whether you pay it monthly, quarterly, or annually. After each bill, assign one of the following two types:

1. Fixed - The amount I pay is set and doesn't change from one billing period to the next. Common examples include rent and cable.

2. Variable - These are expenses and bills that fluctuate from month to month. Common examples include gas for cars and utilities.

Congratulations! You should now have all your accounts and bills listed. Take a breath as you have made a lot of progress. The next step is to determine if you have the accounts required to effectively manage your finances. Here are the key accounts you will need:

1. Core Checking/Debit Account - This is the account your paychecks are deposited into, and it is the account you pay bills from.

2. Expense Curve Savings Account - This account holds savings for upcoming planned expenses.

3. Relationship Insurance Savings Account - This is a "break glass in case of emergency" savings account.

4. Investment Account(s) – I will leave the detailed discussion on investment accounts to the side. Again, my goal is to help you get your personal finances in order so you can be in a position to invest.

Before you go any further, you need a solid understanding of what role each account plays in your new money-management process.

Financial Accounts 101

Your core checking account is the one account we're all familiar with. It is where you have the most activity and where paychecks are deposited. This should be the account you use to pay your bills. A note to anyone paying fees for a checking account or even getting charged ATM fees. Although not required to start this process, you should add finding a new bank account to the to-do list if you are being charged monthly for checking and savings accounts. Doing so may save you $20 a month or more meaning this book pays for itself in just one month. There are many local, regional, and national financial institutions out there to choose from that don't charge account or ATM fees. For now, the key point is to have one account where your income is coming in and your bills are being paid from. In addition, you need to have one core account, not two or seven. Many couples find they have several core accounts but only use one. Simplify your finances and go to one core account. Make sure it is the best fit with easy access to your money, and keep looking until you find one that is free or as close to free as possible.

Next is the expense curve savings account. This account is where the magic happens. On the surface, this is just a basic savings account. The account should be with the same financial institution where you have your core checking account. It is imperative to be able to move money often and easily between the core checking and expense curve savings account. The purpose of this account is to collect regular contributions to infrequent expenses in order to flatten your expense curves. The chart below shows typical expense and income curves, as an annual snapshot with months on the X axis and dollar amounts on the Y axis. This demonstrates how income and expenses vary from month to month. The couple below receives a bonus in March, typically takes a summer vacation in July, and has a spike in expenses during the December holidays.

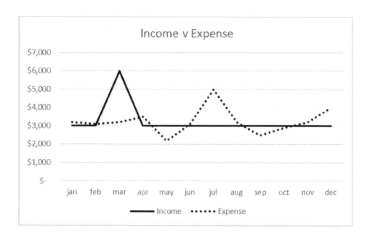

To build your own curve, download the template from my website. On the income side, most people are paid equally every week, twice a month, or even monthly. Chart your income and note which months you typically receive extra income. Added income could be an annual bonus or tax return. These additions will be the spikes in your income curve. If you are paid a variable income, you should estimate income based on previous years. For those on commission and variable income plans, it is always best to take a conservative view on potential income as it is always easier to find places to spend the extra money than cut expenses. As you see from the example above, this couple makes about $3,000 per month with a bonus in March. Like most couples, monthly expenses fluctuate so it is important to get a feel for your own expense line.

You will likely struggle a bit to define your expense curve. You don't have to be exact. This exercise is more about visualizing how much variation between money coming in and money going out, for a given month. It also helps you see which months you have the widest gap between your income and expenses. The easiest way to do this exercise is to use the template on my website. Once you download the template, start with January and go month by month listing one-time expenses that fall within the month. Here we're not looking for the heating bill or a car payment, instead we're trying to capture expenses like vacations, holiday spending, gym memberships, and seasonal and home expenses like snow removal or lawn maintenance.

One way to make the list is to scan your checking or debit account for those one-time charges. For many, your credit card statements will tell the story. What about your daughter's birthday party, back-to-school shopping, skiing, or pool memberships? List each month and note the significant expenses that are above the normal monthly expenses you pay. Don't aim for perfection as you can fine tune the list each month. List the expenses by the month they typically occur and then in the next column, divide the expense by twelve.

Finally, the last column is the number of months between the current month and the month that expense is going to occur. The magic is in learning to see the one-time or infrequent expenses that cause spikes in your expense curve. As you see from the template, the key is flattening spikes by breaking those expenses into twelve payments that you will be making over the year. A basic example is your summer vacation. Assume you spend $2,000 each July to rent a beach house and spend another $1,000 during that week. You would take the total cost of $3,000 for the vacation and divide by twelve. Each month, you need to move $250 into your short-term savings account so you don't put next year's vacation on a credit card. You'll need to gather some more information before you can fully map out your expense curve, but having these infrequent but large known expenses documented is critical.

To state the obvious, if your income and expense curves were always in sync, this personal finance stuff would be simple. Each month you would earn enough to cover your expenses and you wouldn't be reading this book. The reason most people find it difficult to manage their personal finances is that they don't flatten the spikes in their expense curves. In my sample chart, many couples get their bonus check in March and don't look ahead and see their expense spikes. Couples who win with money review their spending plan for March and then consider what large expenses are out there in the coming months. They realize they need to allocate the extra bonus money to offset spikes in their expense curves. You can't expect to win with money if you constantly wait until December to figure out how you are going to pay for holiday gifts. The expense-flattening account is the key to managing your expenses and being prepared for the months when expenses spike. We'll talk more about the mechanics used to manage this account in a bit.

Next you have the relationship insurance savings account. This is an emergency savings account that adds some cushion between your relationship and life. The sole purpose of this account is to build some savings that allows you to sleep better and be more confident in your decision making. When you have savings and a cushion, there will be less stress in your relationship. This savings also protects against having to pull cash from retirement accounts and incurring significant fees and penalties. Reaching into a retirement account (before you are retired) or worse, borrowing money from a relative creates a lot of added complexity, cost, and stress.

We'll talk more about this relationship insurance savings account shortly. This relationship insurance continues to be my favorite hidden gift. I wrote this paragraph on a last-minute flight to visit my grandfather who was hospitalized the day before with life-threatening issues. Having relationship insurance means I booked the flight, my wife and I knew we had the money to and I was free to focus on being with my grandfather and not stressing about the cost of the flights. I can't overstate the importance of investing in this account and insuring your relationship against money fights amid emotionally draining situations. When life happens, you'll be thankful you have this relationship insurance money set aside.

Finally, there are your investment accounts. These are the accounts you will use to invest in your future. For most couples, getting the first three accounts in order enables the focus on this fourth account(s). Until you are in control of your money today, this week, this month, and this year, focusing on investments is a distraction. Walk before you run. I made the choice not to focus my energy helping couples invest. There are many different ways to get investment advice and I hope you all follow my process and begin to create margin in your finances. Use that extra money to invest and fuel your dreams.

As you finish this first session, you should have accomplished the following:

- You created an inventory of all your financial accounts.

- You created your expense and income chart giving you a good feel for your normal income versus expense activity.
- You have a basic understanding of the various accounts you'll need to manage your finances.

It is now time to set up your financial dashboard. The first decision is to define your time period. To keep it simple, most couples plan for two pay periods, usually a four-week duration. If you get paid monthly, you can also just simplify the process and go with monthly periods. Sticking with the four-week period example, you are going to build your first dashboard to include two paychecks (income) and expenses for that given period.

Start by downloading a copy of the financial dashboard template from my website. The dashboard has eight sections. Walk through the template to make sure you are clear on the purpose of each. It is imperative to understand the big picture before jumping into the details and adding in your data. Here is a quick review of each section:

1. Income - This captures the planned income for the current period. This is all the money coming in during the period.
2. Fixed Expenses - These are expenses you typically pay every month. They are usually fixed amounts and only change when you make large financial decisions like buying a house or a new car.

3. Variable Expenses - This is the meat of your dashboard and includes expenses that are typically paid every period but amounts vary.

4. Expense Curve Spikes - This is your secret financial weapon. These expenses occur infrequently but need to be partially funded in the current period.

5. One-time Expenses - These are exception expenses you will only have to pay this period and don't occur normally in a given year.

6. Notes and Action Items Section - Use this section to remember the details you discussed and note any action items you need to follow-up on for the next meeting.

7. Expense Summary Chart - This table shows you a summarized expense view by type for the given period.

8. Balance Amount - This one cell shows money in versus money out for a given period. This one number will tell you if you can afford to spend what you plan to spend in the current period.

For this first period, take it slow and begin by filling out each section. It will take several months to get into a rhythm so work together and focus on really listening to each other. You will look back on these first few months and be surprised how much you learned about your spending. With the high-level review complete, you need to walk through the following steps to complete your first dashboard.

Picking the right time to meet is paramount. Do not try to build your financial dashboard two weeks into a four-week period. You will have already spent money without a plan making it nearly impossible to proactively plan your spending. Ideally, you sit down the evening before you get paid. This will be your primary budget meeting with a check-in meeting scheduled for halfway through the current period. I can't emphasize this point enough. Put these meetings your calendars and protect that time.

As detailed in the template, here are the steps to building your first dashboard.

Step 1 – Add your income to the income section. If you are a two-income family, add both incomes for the current period. After adding your income, add any one-time income expected during this period. Examples of one-time income could be a bonus check, tax return, or birthday money from your parents. *Key takeaway:* this step is usually very easy to complete and allows you to start with a clear view on how much money is going to come in during this period.

Step 2 – Add your fixed expenses for the month. Since this is your first dashboard, you are adding items to this list. These amounts are not going to change frequently so you shouldn't have to spend a lot time on this section during future periods. It should only take you a minute to confirm the amounts are the same. *Key takeaway:* this step is going to show you how much of your income is going toward expenses you have limited ability to change in the next few weeks. These expenses are usually tied to long-term financial commitments.

Step 3 – Add in your variable expenses and set each at your expected spend level for the current period. For example, gas and food are two common variable expenses. Based on your travel and driving plans for the current period, how much gas money will you need? Same for food. How many times are you going to the grocery store? Are you planning to eat at a restaurant? Do you have company coming to stay requiring extra trips to the store? Ask these questions as you estimate your variable expenses. As the periods go by, you will get very good at figuring out how much money you should allocate for each of these expense types. *Key takeaway:* When this section is complete, you have a list of expenses you have significant control over.

Step 4 – Add the contributions for the expense curve expenses. This is where the magic happens. Here you are allocating 1/12 of the expected expense. Although these expenses are not likely due this period, they are real and you need to fund them each period to truly control your spending. If any of the expenses are due this month, you need to note that in the outflow column. *Key takeaway:* Now you have a feel for how much you need to save each period to support some of your larger one-time expenses like vacations and memberships.

Step 5 – Add any one-time expenses. These are truly one-time exceptional expenses. List each and consider if they could have been planned for or deserve an expense category. For example, if you need $100 for your cousin's wedding, you are probably better off creating a large gifts expense curve item and just allocate some money to large gifts each month. *Key takeaway:* One-time expenses are going to be planned for and if you start seeing this expense show up in future periods, you need to move it over to an expense curve item and start funding it on a regular basis.

As you complete the template, you will be able to compare your income versus your expenses. Keep in mind, this dashboard is showing you not only what expenses are due this month but how you are starting to fund larger expenses that will be due in future months. Make sure you consider all expense categories. This includes adding a line for gas or commuter expenses. Add food or grocery expenses, dry cleaners, and gym memberships. You need to include it all to allocate the spending for the month. For many of these categories, you may not even know how much you spend each month. Take a guess and allocate an amount to start the process.

Stop here and admire the work you've done so far. You have a starting point for your dashboard. You can now be confident in how much income will come in this period, what your fixed and variable expenses are, and how much money you have left to pay off debt or other priorities in a given period.

Before you move on, consider how the current month impacts your ability to flatten your spikes in expenses during the upcoming year. To illustrate, assume it is January and you know you typically spend $1,000 during the holidays. To be sure you don't get to December without having set aside money for the holidays, you need to allocate about $80 each period to pay for holiday expenses for the upcoming holidays. Just divide your target amount by twelve and you get the amount you need to save each period. The challenge comes if your first dashboard month is October and you only have three months to save $1,000 for the holidays. Your first year is going to be challenging as you likely haven't planned for all your expenses. That said, if you have six months before the holidays, you may have to double your allocation, but once you hit January, you can reduce your holiday allocation back to 1/12. Spend some time looking at your most challenging expense curves, and work together on a strategy to cover them in the first 12 months.

As you finish this second session, you should have accomplished the following:

- You created your first financial dashboard and have a spending plan for the current period.
- You can see how your expected income fits with expected expenses to evaluate where you will finish the first period. You know how you have to spend your money to live within your means for the next period.

With your initial dashboard loaded with your data, it's time to see how well your financial engine is running. The balance amount is the place to start making adjustments. Ideally, your balance amount is showing a positive number, meaning you have additional income to allocate in the upcoming period. If it is a negative number, you need to follow a different path.

If you have a positive balance, you can make progress paying down debt. If you are debt free, you can start putting money into your investment accounts. Before debt and investments, make sure you fund your relationship insurance savings account. Here you should have a comfortable savings buffer to cover at least two months of living expenses. Next you should pay down and eliminate debt. Identify all your debts and list from smallest to largest. Most people prefer to see progress by paying off the smaller balances first, but math suggests you should pay-off the debts with the highest interest rates first. Maybe you owe mom and dad and prefer to make that your top priority. You decide the order, but be deliberate in paying down debt. Remember paying down debt frees up future income and reduces interest payments, giving you more money to spend and invest.

Once you have funded relationship insurance and you have paid down debt, you should be developing an investing plan. There are many resources to help you develop your investment plan so I only have one piece of advice. Make sure you fully understand what investments you are putting you money into. You should be very clear on what the investment is, what the risks are, and you should be clear on what the historic returns have been. As you consider investing in retirement, paying for college, or any other big investments, spend the time to find an advisor or financial services company you trust. After your investment categories are covered, use excess income to go back and increase any variable expenses you want to expand on this period. Maybe you add more money to your food budget to cover restaurants. Depending on what you prioritize, you might add more to your clothing or travel/vacation fund for this period. Having extra money is a great problem to have, but my guess is you wouldn't still be reading this book if you had too much money. So, let's talk about what to do when your balance amount is a negative number.

When your final balance number is negative, start by reducing the projected spend in your variable expenses. Can you spend less on food, restaurants, or clothing over the next period? Keep in mind, you are focused on the current period, typically four weeks to a month. This exercise is about breaking down the marathon into much smaller pieces. If you are struggling and feeling overwhelmed, try living within a plan for one period. Have confidence that making some sacrifices will make a big difference, and you will end the current period much better off (and in more control) than you have been in many years.

After you get a better feel for your variable expenses, you may find you are forced to cut back on contributing to covering future expenses. If you don't contribute this month for one of your upcoming large expenses, understand that you are increasing the financial strain you will face when that expense comes due. As you start this process, your goal should be to set a realistic allocation of your income to see if you can win with money over the next four weeks. Depending on your situation, that may mean you won't make a lot of progress paying down a credit card balance, but the goal is to get control. Like starting a new fitness program, the first few workouts can be very challenging. Expect a few bumps, but know that it will get easier as you get into a rhythm and gain full control of your finances.

Let's step back and look at the big picture. As you tune your dashboard, listen to what it is telling you. It all starts with considering how much your large fixed expenses impact your spending. Examples like rent or a mortgage combined with car payments are a good place to start. Consider if these big financial commitments impact your overall discretionary income. Do they leave enough room for your other expenses? Your dashboard will help you evaluate if your large fixed expenses are too high. I don't recommend making any rash decisions in the first few months, but many people find their first few dashboards help them understand if they can afford their rent or current car payment. If you can't quickly make changes to the big-ticket items in your budget, a good first step is to commit to not buying any more cars or getting into a more expensive apartment. Take time to get control of your financial world and have confidence in how much you can truly afford.

Your dashboard will give you a clear snapshot of your expenses. If you complete your first dashboard and there is more money going out than coming in, it is time to challenge every expense. Start with the easy expenses. Call your cable company and tell them you need a lower price. Be up front and let them know you are reducing your expenses and need them to help you find a less expensive plan. It was one of the first calls I made, and I was surprised to find out how easy it was to find some savings. Food and restaurants are another common budget buster. Reducing your dining out and even switching to lower cost grocery stores can save hundreds of dollars every month. Make it a challenge to see how much money you can save across your expenses in the first month. Eating at home often translates into healthier food, and that can also be good for the waistline.

Don't miss a key piece of the income puzzle. For many couples, adding a part-time job can make a big difference. It doesn't have to be a fast food job. Get creative. You would be amazed at how many parents need gap coverage in child care and are willing to pay a lot of money to have someone watch their children just before and after school. What about part-time online work? When you focus on your dashboard, you begin to see the value of how part-time and side jobs can make a big impact in your budget. Instead of feeling like the side job is just throwing money at a big financial mess, you will see that additional income having an immediate impact. This is a true hidden gift and one that motivates people to feel more empowered to ask for a raise and to demand more from themselves and their careers.

Beyond reducing expenses and increasing income, this is a good time to remind you to simplify. As I've noted previously, trying to win with money using three accounts and four credit cards is not going to work. Stop working harder and work smarter. Close the old store credit credits and consolidate your bank accounts to a no-fee option. Start with the low-hanging fruit. Consolidate and close accounts. Remove as much financial transaction noise as possible. The simple example is gas or transit expense. Most people spend approximately the same amount on gas or mass transit each month. You can simplify your financial life by spending the money at the beginning of the month. If you are a subway rider, buy the monthly pass. If you allocate $400 in gas per month, take $400 out of the bank at the beginning of the month and put in into an envelope you call the "gas" envelope. Like my grandma used to do, when you need gas, you use the money from the gas envelope. If you are married and have two cars, split the gas money into two envelopes, one for each car. If you just can't do cash, then maybe purchase a refillable gas card from your favorite station. The key is to spend the money up front and do not finish the month with twenty small gas charges on your debit card and three other charges on your credit card. If you don't slow down the amount of swipes and transactions you generate, aka "your digital exhaust," you will need a full-time accountant to keep your financial dashboard up to date.

Consider the idea of using cash and managing expenses via a paper envelope. This is where most couples need to start. Consider it a financial diet that helps you slow down your spending and get control. Speaking from more than ten years of using envelopes, cash can make all the difference. I know the world is moving away from cash, but putting a fixed amount of money in a clothing envelope and only using that clothing envelope in the store will stop you from buying clothes you don't have money for. You may find it so powerful that you won't go back to swiping debit cards for every purchase.

If you are unsure about envelopes, try picking a few variable expense categories in your first cycle and fund them with cash in an envelope. You are likely to find food and grocery is one of your biggest variable expenses. Since food can be purchased in a store (may require cooking and doing dishes) or at a restaurant, I suggest you manage both of them under one category. Consider starting your period with food and grocery money in an envelope, and use the cash in the envelope for all food expenditures. It will not only help you see how much you are spending in this category but also reduce the number of financial transactions you'll have to review at the end of the period. I can attest that handing over cash in restaurants makes you think more about your spending than signing credit card slips. I also find cash makes me enjoy a meal more. I don't worry if I'm overspending or have guilt about my restaurant experience. I know how much money we have for food and we manage to that amount. That said, if you are in week two of four and your food envelope is empty, you need to allocate more to food or consider reducing trips to restaurants.

Cash is going to make your budget meetings much easier. Using your debit card three times per day is going to require you to classify ninety transactions to close out the period. I just won't spend the time adding up all the small transactions, and my guess is you will lose track and fall back into your old ways and lose control. You can also simplify your process of paying bills. Put fixed expenses on auto-pay, and use the last few minutes of you budget meeting to make sure all bills for the current period are paid or you at least set a date to pay them. As a busy father of three with demands on my time every night, I would not be able to stay organized and in total control if I was sliding my debit card four times a day. I have had to find ways to roll frequent transactions into larger buckets to eliminate a lot of the noise from my checking account. Using cash and keeping in envelopes is a new habit and new behavior, so it will take several months to get comfortable so commit to the process. The good news is you can use the test-and-learn approach. Each month or period, you can tweak your dashboard and try different levels of spending levels for various categories. Before you know it, 80 percent of your budget will be on auto-pilot and you'll be spending your budget meetings focused on the other 20 percent. If you know how to manage spreadsheets, have fun with the template and make it work for you. Create categories and tweak the spreadsheet to work for your life.

As you finish this third session, you should have accomplished the following:

- You have tweaked your dashboard to align expected spending to expected income.
- You clearly see if you are living within your means.
- You are starting to get a feel for which specific types of expenses are your most challenging to manage.
- You are exploring options like using cash to help simplify your finances.
- You have a dashboard which can be monitored during the current period and copied to use for subsequent periods.

The New Habit – Communication Is the Key

Communication is at the heart of why this process works and is the greatest gift most couples say comes from the process. You need to consistently meet at the start of your budget cycle so block the time on your calendars for the next twelve months. If evenings are tough, pick a time in the morning when the house is quiet and you can focus. Find a time when you feel energized and don't relegate budget time to fringes of your busy schedule. Don't meet when you are hungry, tired, in the middle of, just starting, or not quite finished arguing about some other issue. Have a strategy and be ready for when the emotional issues surface. Beware that these budget meetings may initially spark difficult discussions as you are forced to prioritize where you will spend your money before you spend the money. Know that controlling your spending from day to day is what enables you to have confidence you can go after your bigger goals and dreams.

So how much time and energy are required to make this work? Your first few budget meetings are going to be emotionally draining. You'll be using muscles you never used before and thinking about your spending in new ways. So take advantage of the energy you'll need to break through the inertia. For some, you've been doing your form of planning for years so give yourself time to get into the new process. The first few months are the hardest. Your first budget meetings can last several hours. Try to make them enjoyable. If you can, find some privacy at your local coffee shop or a small conference room at your library. Bring your laptop or iPad, and have your log in information for accounts so you can gather all the required information. Lastly, take breaks. If it has taken several years for you to get into a disorganized financial pattern, give yourself several blocks of time to create your first budget spreadsheet. The good news is once you get into the routine, planning meetings should only take an hour or less.

The objective of the first budget meeting is to close last period's dashboard. You will need to review your transactions and be sure that your spending matched your plan. If it didn't match, add your transactions into the proper categories and debrief on where you were over and under your spending. Let's be clear that there shouldn't be surprises unless you set your budget and then didn't have a way to control your spending. This gets back to using envelopes to simplify your spending. Once you update the dashboard for the previous period, you will copy the tab and create a new tab. There are some specific steps you need to follow so please review the instructions on the instructions tab of the template. Once you have the new period ready, you use a copy of your dashboard from last month as a starting point for the next period. You will adjust your income and expected spending in each category. You should leave the first meeting with your spending plan finalized for the upcoming period.

The second meeting happens halfway through your current period. This should be a brief meeting to review your financial transactions from the first half of the month and ensure you are on schedule. If you find that you are struggling to keep the dashboard updated with just two meetings, you can meet each week. I prefer to stick to just two meetings a month so review the steps for simplifying your financial life. If you are trying to classify fifty transactions or charges, consider using more cash and the envelope system. If you are swiping your debit card five times a day, you are going to need a master's degree in accounting to make sense of the spending.

Most couples find they run into a few major hurdles so be ready for these and know what you need to do to get over them.

Pitfall 1 – Over-complicating the system. If you are spending using four credit cards, two debit accounts, and three checkbooks, you need to streamline your financial accounts so you can have a clear picture of your money and spending.

Pitfall 2 – Not holding to your meeting schedule or waiting until the current period has started to plan your budget. You must make time for the budget meeting before the money hits your account and you start spending. If you go with the standard one full budget meeting at the start of the period and a shorter mid-period check-in, you can't afford to skip those meetings. You can delay the meeting a day or two, but be careful to not start spending into your current budget cycle without having the spending plan in place

Pitfall 3 – Blending categories. You allocated your spending by category so don't undermine the whole process by mixing and matching categories. If you allocated gas money and decide to use that money to buy shoes, you'll probably finish the month with gas charges on your credit card and shoes you don't need. Couples need to pay special attention to this pitfall. If you allocated $100 this month to clothes, you need to either keep that $100 in cash in a clothing envelope you share with your partner or communicate to your partner that you just bought a new $75 shirt on your debit card and that means you only have $25 left to spend on clothing this month.

Communication is key. Putting cash into an envelope at the beginning of a period simplifies this process. Cash may seem old fashioned, but if you know overspending on clothing is your weakness, put yourself on the cash clothing plan. Yes, that means you may need to give up your favorite store charge card. Let those "points" and "benefits" from the charge card programs go. Simplify your life, and be assured that any savings you would get from being a member or reward club on charge cards will come back to you tenfold as you never pay interest or late fees again. Stores make more off credit accounts than what is in your shopping cart. That explains why you need to say no every time you are offered those store credit cards. No, I don't want to save 25 percent today by signing up for a credit card. Simplify your life and say no!

My hope is that you find the process smooth sailing from the beginning, but be prepared for a few storms. You can work together to get through them. Next, let's take a closer look at what budget love looks like in action.

Enjoying Budget Love

*"People rarely succeed unless they have fun
in what they are doing." - Dale Carnegie*

What does budget love look like? I enjoy going to my local sports store and buying a new pair of Nike sneakers. They practically jump off the shelf when I walk by. Budget love is defined in that moment you are holding those Nikes, approaching the register about to pull out your debit card. Budget love is about loving yourself and your partner enough to stop in that moment to consider the question. Did we plan for this purchase? Do we have money in the clothing fund this month? If yes, budget love says to buy those new shoes and wear them with no regrets. You own them and won't be making an 18 percent interest payment that turns that great deal into a $300 pair of sneakers. Enjoy the shopping experience.

What if the answer was no and you didn't have enough in the clothing budget this month? Budget love is caring enough about yourself and your partner to consider the bigger goals you are trying to achieve and putting those shoes back on the shelf.

Budget love may mean you slipped even further and bought the shoes. Budget love means you put those shoes back in the bag, drive back to the store, and return them for a full refund. Some would suggest I'm taking the fun out of shopping, and budget love is restrictive. Rethink this scenario and consider which decision is most liberating. Being true to your plan and achieving your financial goals. The alternative is to overspend, pay interest each month on a pair of shoes you really don't need, and live under the weight of constant financial stress. What about the impact to your relationship when one partner, or worse both, are not willing to be adults and recognize you only have so much money coming in every month? If you've been overspending every month, consider how liberating it would be to live without the stress of debt. You rob yourself of the joy of shopping when you can't afford something and have to live with buyer's remorse.

Planning your spending changes everything. You move from a position of uncertainty to one of control and confidence to enjoy your purchase. I can attest that returning something that you wanted but was not accounted for in your spending plan is incredibly hard but empowering. There is tremendous power in that first experience when you fall but get back up again and bring the shoes back, say no to the credit card, or close that browser before hitting the confirm purchase button. The focus will shift from that one thing you think you needed to the bigger goals you have for your relationship. Your relationship, your dreams, and your sanity are worth more than overspending to buy the next cool gadget or piece of clothing!

Budget love can also motivate you in two ways you would not have expected. First, step back to that moment you are in the store and you had to have the $60 shoes. You open your clothing envelope and you find there is only $50 in the envelope. You will quickly become very resourceful. You might decide to search online for a coupon or ask the clerk if there are any store or online discounts this week. You will be surprised how often you find ways to save money. Even when it comes to services, from car repairs, appliance purchases, and house repairs, you can negotiate lower prices when you have money ready to spend and don't need to obtain credit to pay for the service. Be transparent with a vendor. Share what your budget is, and challenge them to help get the project or product within your budget. You will be surprised how often people are willing to flex their price, find an extra coupon, or give you a one-time discount. Notice that I didn't advise you to sign up for the credit card.

Once you establish your new routine, you will begin to feel a sense of control. You will feel good about having a plan and spend less time stressing about finances. You also may find you go from stressing about things you should not have purchased to spending more time planning on how you can afford that which you want to purchase. As an individual or couple, be prepared for new doors to open along this journey. Your financial dashboard will begin to show you that each dollar is equal. For some,, that means you call the cable company and negotiate a new rate saving $20 a month. Before your dashboard, you wouldn't bother chasing a $20 a month discount but that ten-minute phone call could generate $20 extra to pay down debt or give you a little more room in your clothing allocation each month. Depending on how expensive your tastes for shoes, that one phone call is worth a new pair of shoes every three months. When your finances are disorganized, you lose out on a lot of smaller opportunities to get more from your income. When you constantly use credit to purchase things, you are less likely to negotiate on price and less likely to search for a coupon or online deal.

Getting your finances in order will bring clarity to financial decisions you made in the past while informing the next big purchase. How much are your cars costing you? Americans have become accustomed to new cars every few years as the norm. As you track your spending, you may decide owning a car for more than five years has a major impact on your ability to spend money on other wants such as travel or even to fund your early retirement. As you organize your finances, you might begin to question if it is time to cut the cord, shop for new internet service, or price shop for new insurance. You may find that doing some extra laundry and ironing at home saves large dry cleaner bills, and you still look great at work. I can constantly upgrade my work wardrobe just by eliminating my dry-cleaning bill. Lawn care or snow removal is another example where you might elect to buy a riding mower as a more cost-effective way to take care of your lawn. I'm not one for telling you what the right answers are for you, but doing your monthly budget should get you asking the right questions, questions that only you and your partner can prioritize. If you hate doing laundry and love getting nice clean shirts each week, prioritize that service. The challenge for most of us is that we won't be able to afford all the various services that make our lives easier - thus, the need to prioritize and be realistic during budget meetings.

The ultimate example of budget love can come at the darkest and most difficult days. Too often a partner gets sick or even dies and the remaining partner is unprepared to manage their finances. When both partners are involved in the monthly discussions, both individuals know what the current financial picture is, and where money is being spent and saved. As difficult as a serious illness or death of a partner can be, budget love is caring enough about each other to leave the one you love without a financial mess. We all know stories where a partner is sick or dies, and the remaining partner is left to dig through mountains of papers and account statements to sort out finances. Worse, some couples who have not managed their finances well take the financial stress and burden shared by two people and leave that burden on the shoulders of the remaining partner. Too often, traditional roles meant the men did the finances and women just trusted them. I'm all about trusting each other, but couples need to know how to manage their finances and be clear where they are on their financial journey. As you have learned, if you follow this process, you won't leave random accounts with bits and pieces of your financial activity for someone else to try to piece together. If you have designated a family member or a friend to take care of your financial affairs after your death, I suggest you show them your financial spreadsheet or at a minimum, let them know where to find the latest copy so they can step in and drive.

Budget love also puts an accurate price tag on your lifestyle. When you break down your spending and plan spending across a given year, you understand what it costs to maintain your lifestyle. Do you know how much you spend on gas or food? Most people never take the time to answer these basic questions. You need to know what your normal expenses are so you know what it costs to live your lifestyle. The budgeting process goes beyond covering current period expenses to plan and prepare for your next vacation and the holidays. This process will give you clarity into short-term spending with visibility into meeting long-term goals. Budget love prepares for the unexpected. What If you find out tomorrow that your company is moving and you're losing your job? Your financial dashboard gives you a snapshot to make informed financial decisions. Don't wait until the day the surprise hits to figure out your plan. Losing a job or getting hit with an unexpected large expense is never easy, but don't make it harder by not having financial tools to make the best financial decisions.

Budget love is also always being ready to make the most of a financial gift. Couples who are not controlling their spending will look back on the gift and wonder how they spent the money. If you struggle with managing your spending, don't fool yourself into thinking an influx of money will solve your problems. Long-term financial success starts with a budget and prioritizing your spending. Budget love is being ready to accept a financial gift and honoring the giver by maximizing that gift in your life.

Speaking of financial gifts, a favorite benefit of budget love comes from the old saying "I learned it from you, Mom and Dad!" Fill in the blank for your childhood. My mom and dad always "blank" when it came to money. If you have children or hope to in the future, they will be watching. I want to encourage you to model constructive communication and budget love for your children. Depending on the ages of your children, you should agree on how much detail you want to share, but I'd argue the details don't really matter. If you follow this process, the gift you'll find is your modeling how to constructively and proactively manage your finances. Your children will see you making it a priority to plan your spending and will see their parents working through financial decisions together. I'm not proposing you discuss the detailed dollar amounts in your budget, but emphasize the process. Schedule a few budget meetings when the kids are around, and they will see you working on a financial plan. Use purchases to remind your children that you planned for this type of expense or you didn't and therefore can't buy it this month.

In our house, we like to demonstrate disagreement on priorities. What happens when mom and dad don't agree on the spending plan for the upcoming month? And, yes, this will happen frequently! Let your kids see mom and dad working through these difficult decisions and modeling how to compromise. Our children will never hear the following from either of us: "Don't tell mom that I spent" or "If your father found out." Not going to happen in our house. What our kids hear instead is: "Mom and Dad don't keep secrets from each other except for gifts and surprise parties." We are tested constantly by our children, and we are a unified front. The older our children get, the more certain they can be on this boundary. Pass it on. I am convinced that teaching our children how to manage money is more important than passing on a big inheritance. If you have the choice to give them a fish or teach them to fish, teach them to fish and they will prosper.

Now for my closing argument on why you should chase budget love with abandonment. Budget love enables you to make a difference beyond your own lives. I hope this new process helps you build intimacy in your relationship, to grow closer, and see your family prosper. With the solid financial foundation, budget love will set you free to help others in need, from your sibling caught in a crisis or the child thousands of miles away who is stuck in poverty. We often read about the big donation to a local university by very wealthy people. These donations are amazing examples, but I don't think you should aspire to them as you begin this journey. Start with an amount that you can contribute each month and find a worthy cause. As you plan, use your dashboard to prioritize and identify an option to have a major impact on a specific target audience. A common first step could be to sponsor a child and help give them a chance to attend a better school. For just $30 per month, you can dramatically change the course of the life of child. Maybe your passion is dogs, cats, or dolphins. Find a group that is doing good work for whatever animal you love, and make a regular commitment to them. Your contribution will make a difference, and you can begin to build a legacy of giving that can transform lives. This is not a guilt trip but an invitation to consider what new doors will open in your life and in your heart when you achieve full control of your finances.

Budget loves opens doors that you'll never regret walking though.

Taking It to the Next Level

"If you gave up, you've already lost. If you keep going, you get to a new level." - Lyoto Machida

As you work your financial plan, the fog around your financial future will begin to lift. You are going to have clear visibility into how you spend money. The budget process will help you manage your finances in smaller chunks of time. It will help you stop driving with the rearview mirror and shift toward proactive planning. What follows are some examples of proactive steps you can take to further move the needle and help you reach your goals. Take it to the next level. I'll start with the easy items, and we'll progress into deeper waters.

Focus on fixed expenses. Are there any options you can offer me to reduce my bill while remaining a loyal customer? With one phone call, you can save $20 dollars or more each month. The old me would read this paragraph and think, "Who cares about $20 a month?" I've seen the light, and I know that $20 a month is $240 a year and that adds up to

$2,400 over the next ten years. Don't tell me you don't have any money to invest and save for the future if you haven't called your cable company lately. Go through each of your fixed expenses, and challenge each one.

Don't make the mistake of assuming you can't impact a fixed expense. If you work for an organization that has a budget – a company, a school, a nonprofit, it means applying the same expense management you would apply at work to your personal budgets. When is the last time you called your landlord and suggested a new lease? Even if you are in month four of a twelve-month lease, you can be creative. Assuming you want to stay, call the landlord, tell them how much you like the place, remind her how great of a tenant you are. Next, ask if she would be willing to extend the lease twelve more months at $50 discount per month. You give your landlord security while helping avoid the usual annual increase in rent. What is the worst your landlord could say? She could say no, but I know a lot of landlords who value a good tenant over making an extra $50 a month. Try it, and have fun celebrating these small victories.

Taking it to the next level means considering if you have any sacred cows. For those of you who "own" a home, that may be the elephant in the budget room. Start running some searches on the web, make some phone calls, and challenge your current interest rate. You may find that you can reduce your mortgage from a thirty to fifteen year and take advantage of a lower rate. This was a massive win in our house. When the day came and we signed the final papers on our refinanced mortgage, I danced around my kitchen. I hope you find something to dance about as you go through this process.

Hang on for this next one as I'm going to lose some you. Some of you need to consider slaying the financial monster eating your income. For most families, the monster is hiding in your driveway. Vehicles are a typical big-line item in your budget. As you complete your budget, consider how much interest you are paying on your cars. As crazy as this sounds, consider paying off your cars and start paying yourself a car payment. That's right, be your own bank. If you are willing to drive your cars a bit longer, you will be amazed at how good it feels to not have to make car payments and pay interest every month. I'm not going to say much more on this topic but understand a lot of Americans walk around believing everyone has car loans. They don't, and for those who stopped buying cars on credit, you'll seldom find one who misses giving the finance company interest every month for that car. Simplify and pay off the car. Get rid of car payments, and save money for your next car. I'm not judging. Lease or finance a car if that is what you want, but be sure you've considered the impact of the payments and the long-term impact of giving a bank interest every month.

Taking it to the next level also means putting money behind your dreams. Stuck in a job you don't like? Want to take that trip you've always dreamed of? Cash flow it. Start a new category, and put $10 in it this month. Maybe that is all you can afford, go for it, and dare to start down the path with just $25. Maybe next month you add $50 and the third month $75. After three months, you have $150 and you start to want to stretch to make this category grow. Feed the category, and feed your dreams.

I heard a commercial for a personal loan to get that vacation you always wanted and deserved. Vacations are much more relaxing when you don't have to come home and struggle to get the credit card statement dislodged from your mailbox. When you lie in bed that first night back from vacation, you'll feel so much more refreshed if the credit card charges or thirty easy payments are not waiting for you. Go back to your expense curves. If you are a one or two-a-year-vacation family, set your vacation budget and save monthly. There is power in putting that money in the vacation fund at the beginning of every month as you are less likely to blow money on an unplanned dinner at the local restaurant. Consider how much you are going to enjoy the upcoming vacation, and use that power to drive past the restaurant and pick up some pasta and sauce at the grocery store to eat at home.

Focus on reducing fixed expenses, and don't be afraid to go after the big ones, including rent or a mortgage. Consider the financial impact of large car payments and throwing money out the window on interest. Don't put vacations on credit. Scale your vacation back or just give yourself more time to save for the next trip. These are just a few examples of how you can take it to the next level.

About Those Bed Sheets

Financial stress has a way of following you around each day and even as you try to fall asleep at night. Don't waste your time and energy worrying about finances. I wrote this book when I had the epiphany that just an hour or two a month of time spent on the spreadsheet takes away the anxiety and allows your mind to focus on better things.

Unfortunately, most of us walk around thinking it is normal to just live with constant financial stress. You are not sure how the bills are going to get paid, and each month you add a bit more debt. Debts go up, interest payments increase. This monthly battle wages on and then the car needs brakes or a family emergency means you must travel on short notice. You've gone from stressed to dealing with a family and financial crisis. These are the makings of a stressful financial mess that will cause you to fight instead of pulling out your budget and figuring out how to attack this problem. Don't minimize the potential impact financial stress can have on your relationship. Stress pushes couples apart and equates to less quality time between the sheets. Fall asleep with confidence in tomorrow. Time spent in your spreadsheet will mean less time worrying and more time sleeping.

At the end of the day, my hope is this material, this new way of thinking and behaving will give you and your family a chance to cope with financial stress in a new and powerful way. I shared the story of the young boy in the chair sitting in the hallway of his school wondering why his parents don't love each other anymore. Maybe, if the lines of communication could have stayed open, the big arguments about money would never have happened. I won the relationship lottery when I met my wife. Like many of you, I entered marriage knowing that the odds are not in my favor to go the distance. Having been on this journey almost twenty years with my amazing wife, I wrote this book to share one of the most important lessons we have learned. Communication about how and where you spend your money is critical. Communication on the income side is just as important. Do we need to make more money in the form of a potential job offer or does the money we make today enable us to be happy and meet our long-term goals? More is not always the answer, and having a financial plan helps you make the right decision for you and the people you love.

It's time for you to write the next chapter. Being in control of your finances will allow you to get the most out of your career, your relationships, and make you feel better about yourself. It starts with picking a day to begin. That day leads to a week then a month. The months will quickly add up, and the momentum will build. Never forget this budget stuff is not about the money. It is about the impact you can have on your life and those around you.

Now that you found love, invest the time to keep your financial dashboard current, get control, and make your dreams happen.

Made in the USA
Middletown, DE
13 July 2020